HOW POLITICAL CORRECTNESS IS DESTROYING AUSTRALIA

ENEMIES WITHIN AND WITHOUT

DR KEVIN DONNELLY

Published by:
Wilkinson Publishing Pty Ltd
ACN 006 042 173
Level 4, 2 Collins Street
Melbourne, Vic 3000
Ph: 03 9654 5446
www.wilkinsonpublishing.com.au

NATIONAL
LIBRARY
OF AUSTRALIA

A catalogue record for this
book is available from the
National Library of Australia

Planned date of publication: 04-2018
Title: How Political Correctness is Destroying Australia
ISBN(s): 9781925642407 : Printed - Paperback

Design by Tango Media
Printed in Australia

'If you want to know why you should be proud
of Australia, read Kevin Donnelly.'

'Few Australian educators have done as much as
Kevin Donnelly, ideological warrior extraordinaire,
to alert the nation to the dumbing down of curriculum and
green-Left ideological intrusions into Australian classrooms.
His analysis and insights, based on facts and experience, are
always provocative, interesting and worth reading.'

'If we fail to heed Kevin's warnings to reverse the long march
of the cultural Marxists, our nation will be lost. The shades
are fast drawing on our window of opportunity but this book
gives hope that the curtains can be pulled back.'

'Kevin is a passionate advocate for good education and,
more importantly, for children, curriculum reform and good
teaching practice. He defends the Western canon and Judeo-
Christian values, shunning faddish post-modern theory
and its detrimental influence on Australian schools and
universities. He is no friend of cultural relativism and strongly
advocates for higher quality and better paid teachers.
He is of course right.'

Don't you see that the whole aim of Newspeak is to narrow the range of thought? In the end we shall make thoughtcrime literally impossible, because there will be no words in which to express it.

George Orwell,
Nineteen Eighty-Four

DR KEVIN DONNELLY AM

Kevin is a staunch defender of the strengths and benefits of Western civilisation and our Judeo-Christian heritage that is being undermined by the PC movement and is one of Australia's leading conservative commentators and authors.

Opinion pieces have been published in all of Australia's mainstream print and digital media, including: the *Australian*, the *Herald Sun*, the *Daily Telegraph*, the *Courier Mail*, the *Sydney Morning Herald*, the *Age*, *Newsweekly*, *Quadrant Online*, the ABC's *The Drum* and *On Line Opinion*.

Previous publications include: *The Culture of Freedom*, *Why our schools are failing*, *Dumbing Down*, *Australia's Education Revolution*, *Educating your child: it's not rocket science* and *Taming the black dog*.

Kevin taught English and Humanities for 18 years in Victorian government and non-government secondary schools and has also been a member of state and national curriculum bodies, including: the Victorian Board of Studies and the federally funded Discovering Democracy Programme. In 2014 Kevin co-chaired the review of the Australian National Curriculum for the Commonwealth Government.

He is a Senior Research Fellow at the Australian Catholic University and Director of the Education Standards Institute. In the 2016 Queen's Birthday Honours List Kevin was appointed as a Member of the Order of Australia for services to education.

This anthology includes comment pieces previously published in a number of Australian newspapers and current affairs magazines.

CONTENTS

The dangers of Islamic
fundamentalism..80

Safe schools, same-sex marriage and the LGBTQI sexuality and gender agenda 148

FOREWORD

Dr Kevin Donnelly AM is a man of pre-eminence and extraordinary relevance in the current Australian education environment.

He writes and speaks with authority and relevance born of wide experience.

It should be noted that he is a Senior Research Fellow at the Australian Catholic University.

He taught English and social studies for 18 years in Government and non-Government secondary schools and has been a member of State and national curriculum bodies.

He was a branch president of the Victorian Secondary Teachers Association.

He was co-chairman of a 2014 review into the national curriculum.

He is the Director of Education Standards Institute, a company specialising in producing curriculum materials and analysing and benchmarking Australian and international school curriculums.

He is also a former member of the Year 12 English Panel of Examiners, the Victorian Board of Studies and the Discovering Democracy program.

I cite all of the above as proof of the fact that this man, through experience and the articulation of important views on education, deserves to be heard.

But, perhaps more importantly, as a longstanding public commentator, he has opened a window to average Australians allowing them to see what is going on in classrooms and universities today.

It is not a glamorous picture.

Whether the subject was the long-running debate over phonics versus so-called whole word recognition in the teaching of literacy, falling teaching standards, pointless and wasteful education spending, Leftist political correctness or the defence of the moral and spiritual value of the Judeo-Christian tradition we describe as Western civilisation, Kevin Donnelly has always been there, fearlessly expressing his view, along with the often unpalatable facts, in a way the general public can understand.

And dare I say it, the public meets these views with almost universal agreement.

They resonate because they reflect the tried and true principles of classical education and common sense.

A classroom without discipline can't provide education; a teacher without enthusiasm, motivation and a modicum of education can't teach effectively; flexible schools freed from centralised control will invariably achieve better results; an overcrowded curriculum bogged down in the so-called culture wars, trivial identity politics and other tangential subjects does not equate with education.

These are all simple, sensible ideas championed by Dr Donnelly.

How many parents can identify with his following comments?

"Students often spend more time learning to be politically correct than being introduced to our best validated knowledge and artistic achievements."

"Curricula, rather than focus on academically based subjects, force teachers to deal with abstracts."

"Basic skills like memorising times tables and rhymes and poems must become automatic before more difficult and abstract learning can take place."

Dr Kevin Donnelly has also, by virtue of his rejection of political correctness and his celebration of the Judeo-Christian tradition, become a champion of Western civilisation.

His latest book is a powerful response to the threat posed by the cultural-left to Western civilisation; or as I have often argued, a challenge to the march by the left through our institutions.

We can no longer rest on our educational laurels.

It is time to strike a blow in support of genuine education and to challenge the pervasive, destructive erosion of Western values by the Left.

Alan Jones

INTRODUCTION

Similar to what is happening in America, Europe and the UK political correctness is destroying Australia's cultural heritage and what is best about our institutions and way of life. No longer is it possible to acknowledge and celebrate the debt owed to Western civilisation and to argue that Judeo-Christianity and epochal events like the Renaissance, Reformation and the Enlightenment deserve to be praised.

No longer is it possible to celebrate Captain Cook's discovery of what is now Australia, the arrival of the First Fleet or the fact that we are a beacon of liberty and prosperity in what is an increasingly dangerous and hostile world. As a result of the cultural-left's long march through the institutions we are told to feel guilty about of the 'sins of the past' and to accept society is riven with inequality and injustice.

Advocates of multiculturalism argue that we must accept diversity and difference and that all those who come to live here must be accepted and tolerated — no matter how un-Australian their beliefs and values. Those who believe that Western culture is superior or more beneficial compared to other cultures and that Islamic fundamentalism is a threat are labelled Eurocentric, racist and Islamophobic.

Those on the cultural-left committed to a deep green agenda and who worship the Gaia blame global warming on the industrial world's reliance on fossil fuels and argue the only way to save the planet is to ban coal and impose unreliable and costly wind and solar power.

Ignored is the reality that wind and solar power is intermittent and only power sourced from coal, gas and hydro-electricity, that Australia has in abundance, is reliable and more cost effective.

Political correctness is also responsible for restricting free speech and open and dispassionate debate. Everyday conversations and interactions are closely scrutinised by the thought-police to ensure nobody offends in areas like gender and sexuality, ethnicity, physical appearance or social background. Unless, of course, you are a while, middle-class, older male with Christian values and then you are ripe for attack.

The school curriculum teaches students that Western societies are inherently inequitable and unjust and that what constitutes worthwhile knowledge is simply a vehicle imposed by the capitalist class to oppress others. Our universities now teach the evils of 'whiteness' and trigger warnings are imposed to ensure minority and victim groups and individuals do not feel undervalued or threatened by what is taught.

Notwithstanding the billions spent on Indigenous affairs and the High Court's Mabo decision in support of land rights for Aboriginal and Torres Strait Islanders we are told that 'white' Australia is the sole cause of past, current and future injustices. Ignored is the dysfunctional nature of many indigenous communities and the fact, as argued by Noel Pearson, that not all their grievances can be blamed on Western society and our Anglo-Celtic heritage.

Even though thousands in Australia, Europe, the UK, America and Africa and the Middle East have been injured and killed as a result of Islamic terrorism the cultural-left argues that Islam is a peaceful religion.

Ignored, as argued by Ayaan Hirsi Ali, is that parts of the Koran call for a fatwa against the unbelievers and the establishment of an Islamic caliphate and the imposition of sharia law. Those who disagree are subjected to the law of dhimmi — a situation where they are either killed, lose all their political and legal rights or made to convert to Islam.

As argued by the one-time Prime Minister of England David Cameron for far too long cultural-left academics and a sympathetic media have argued events like 9/11, the deaths in Paris and Nice, the London bombings and the Bali bombings that killed so many Australians are the West's fault instead of criticising Islamic fundamentalism.

Proven by the Marxist inspired Safe Schools gender and sexuality program, where children are taught that gender is fluid and limitless and that they, and not their parents, can decide whatever they want to be, political correctness is also undermining the binary nature of gender by ignoring the fact that approximately 99% of babies are born male or female.

In addition to arguing that kindergarten and primary school age children should be taught about the Gender Fairy who has the power to change a boy to a girl and a girl to a boy the Safe Schools material also condemns those who believe that marriage should be between a man and a woman as heteronormative, homophobic and transphobic.

It should not surprise that the radical academic who designed the Safe Schools program, Roz Ward, argues that "only Marxism provides the theory and practice of genuine human liberation" and that the "Safe Schools Coalition is about supporting gender and sexual diversity, not about stopping bullying".

There is an alternative to political correctness and the cultural-left's long march through the institutions. As I argue in the following comment pieces there is much of value and beneficial about Western civilisation and our way of life. Unlike the millions around the world living under the tyranny of totalitarian dictatorships and oligarchies those in the West are guaranteed freedom, liberty and equality before the law.

As a result of Christianity and the New Testament and events like the Glorious Revolution and institutions like Westminster Parliament and English common law those who live in the West are also able to go about their daily lives without unwarranted government intrusion and coercion.

The West is also the world's power house in terms of scientific, medical and technological innovation that enables increased productivity, food production and wealth; ensuring that individuals are healthier and able to enjoy increased life expectancy.

That Western nations like Australia are so successful and attractive explains why so many refugees and immigrants from around the world seek to live here. The irony, of course, is that the very values and institutions that safeguard and protect our way of life and that make this country so attractive and unique are the very things that the cultural-left is seeking to undermine and destroy.

THE CULTURAL-
LEFT'S POLITICALLY
CORRECT LONG
MARCH THROUGH
THE INSTITUTIONS

*The thinkers of the Frankfurt School
revised Marxism as primarily a cultural
rather than an economic movement. In
place of anger at traditional capitalism,
scorn was directed at the reigning
values of the West.[1]*

1   Michael Gove. 2006. *Celsius 7/7*. London. Weidenfield & Nicolson. p 64

Multiculturalism and political correctness are killing Australia

Douglas Murray's book *The Strange Death of Europe* deals with far away countries such as England, France, Germany, Sweden, Italy and Greece but it should be compulsory reading here. Murray argues "Europe is committing suicide" and while the situation in Australia is nowhere near as dramatic we are also in danger.

Similar to Europe, in our own country multiculturalism reigns supreme, we are made to feel guilty about the past and the cultural-left elites label anyone who disagrees as "deplorables".

Murray also writes that modern, secular society where materialism is the new religion ignores the fact that people need a spiritual and moral sense of identity and purpose. Unless Western civilisation rediscovers what gives it identity, confidence and strength then it is signing its own death warrant.

The first catastrophe facing England and Europe is the influx of millions of Islamic refugees over the past five to 10 years. As a result, suburbs in Paris, London and Brussels are no-go zones, Islamic terrorism and crime are weekly events and increasing numbers of locals feel they are strangers in their own land.

Germany, for example, has taken in more than one million refugees since the start of the Syrian civil war while Greece and Italy, whose economies are already suffering, are being inundated with boat people from Turkey and northern Africa.

Whereas Europe has always welcomed immigrants Murray argues that what is different about the latest surge of mainly poorly educated young Muslim men is that many are unable or unwilling to assimilate or, worst of all, hellbent on inflicting violence and death.

And the terrorist attacks and violence will only increase as more and more refugees arrive, or those already living in England and Europe become radicalised.

Forget German Chancellor Angela Merkel's mistaken belief that embracing diversity and difference represents the best way forward. Contrary to the political elites, cultural-left academics and many in the media, Murray argues that multiculturalism is destroying what makes Europe unique.

Murray writes: "By the end of the lifespans of most of the people currently alive, Europe will no longer be Europe and the peoples of Europe will have lost the only place in the world we had to call home."

And the process is well under way. In London Islamic fundamentalists want to introduce sharia law and figures show that more than 10,000 girls under 15 living in England and Wales have been subjected to female genital mutilation.

Such is the parlous state caused by the arrival of thousands and thousands of boat people that many in Europe now argue they should copy John Howard and Tony Abbott and close the borders and refuse to let the refugees land.

The second threat facing Europe, at the same time as Islamic terrorism, is that Europeans are turning their backs on Christianity and Enlightenment ideals that are the foundation stones on which European civilisation depends.

Murray argues that "Europe has lost faith in its beliefs, traditions and legitimacy" when it needs to assert itself against a foreign culture imported by Islamic fundamentalism. In universities and schools, students are taught that there is nothing beneficial or worthwhile about Western civilisation.

Politically correct advocates condemn nations such as England, France and Germany for their colonial past, feminists attack society as misogynist and sexist and neo-Marxists attack capitalism as inequitable and unjust.

Although an atheist, Murray is especially concerned about Christianity being ignored as the New Testament, in particular, provides a strong moral and ethical framework that underpins European institutions and way of life.

As argued by Perth legal expert Augusto Zimmermann, the Ten Commandments and concepts like the inherent dignity of each person and the right to "life, liberty and the pursuit of happiness" are Christian in origin.

Much of Western civilisation's art, literature, music and architecture — including Michelangelo's David, Leonardo da Vinci's The Last Supper, Bach's Mass in B minor and the great cathedrals such St Paul's and Notre Dame — only exist thanks to Christianity.

There is much Australians can learn from Murray's book.

Firstly, like Europe, freedom of speech and the right to speak out against multiculturalism have been lost.

Political correctness rules and anyone critical of immigration is condemned as xenophobic, racist and Islamophobic.

Secondly, in the same way that many condemn Europe for its imperialist past, many in Australia condemn the arrival of the First Fleet and the fact that the nation began as a British colony. In relation to Australia, Murray writes: "Colonialism has become the nation's founding original sin."

And like original sin, all those not of Aboriginal descent must always apologise.

Prompting the question: how long will succeeding generations be made to feel guilty about something that happened 200 years earlier?

Thirdly, similar to Europe, where right-wing parties such as Germany's AfD Party and France's National Front are growing in strength, the resurgence of Pauline Hanson's One Nation

Party and the fact that the Turnbull government is bleeding votes from its conservative base prove that Australians are also fed up with being silenced and ignored.

Sydney University – politically correct and cultural-left

The University of Sydney's latest marketing campaign titled 'Unlearn' beggars belief but provides a striking example of how successful the cultural-left has been in subverting the academy. Forget about Cardinal Newman's ideal of a university education being committed to wisdom and truth and the pursuit of knowledge for its own sake.

While education has always involved questioning accepted truths and challenging the status quo you only need to watch the campaign's accompanying video to realise that what is intended is more about enforcing a politically correct view of the world on students than wisdom and truth.

The video centres on issues championed by the cultural-left, including indigenous land rights, same-sex marriage, world peace, imprisoned refugees and Islamophobia and students are told they have "To be brave enough to question the world, challenge the established, demolish social norms and build new ones in their place".

It should not surprise that the University of Sydney no longer champions what the poet T. S. Eliot describes as "the preservation of learning, for the pursuit of truth, and in so far as men are capable of it, the attainment of wisdom".

Since the cultural revolution of the late '60s and early '70s the more conservative liberal view of education has been attacked and undermined by a rainbow alliance of cultural-left movements including: Marxism, Neo-Marxism, deconstructionism, postmodernism, feminism and post-colonial and LGBTQI theories.

While often in conflict and disagreement what all hold in common is the belief that there are no absolutes as knowledge is simply a socio-cultural construct that reinforces the hegemony of the ruling class.

A liberal education, instead of being inherently worthwhile or beneficial for its own sake, is part of the 'ideological state apparatus' that capitalism uses to reinforce 'false consciousness' and to disempower already marginalised groups.

As noted by the American academic Christopher Lasch, as a result of the cultural-left's long march through the academy, the university curriculum instead of embodying a "universal transcendent truth" is attacked for disguising the self-serving power of "white Eurocentric males".

In history, for example, instead of acknowledging the strengths and benefits of Western civilisation students are taught that Western civilisation is oppressive, misogynist, racist, sexist, elitist and guilty of a myriad of politically incorrect crimes ranging from speciesism to environmental destruction.

One only needs to note the fate of one of Australia's most significant historians, Geoffrey Blainey, who during the mid-1980s was hounded out of Melbourne University for daring to question the rate of Asian immigration and the impact of multiculturalism, to appreciate how successful the cultural-left has been in taking control of the academy.

Omid Tofighian from the University of Sydney provides an example of the cultural-left's critique of a liberal education within the Western tradition. Tofighian argues that the existing university curriculum must be challenged as it privileges

"Eurocentric concepts" and "replicates and reinforces the concept of whiteness".

The concept of "whiteness", so Tofighian argues, leads to "different forms of domination and marginalization — such as racism, sexism, classism, historical injustice and prejudice based on religion".

How literature is now conceived and taught in our universities has also become a victim of the cultural-left's long march. The classics associated with the Western literary canon, instead of being valued for their moral and aesthetic value and because they have something enduring and profound to say about human nature and the world in which we exist, are defined as socio-cultural products.

The English academic Terry Eagleton in his 1983 book *Literary Theory: An Introduction,* in addition to arguing that there is nothing inherently worthwhile or valuable about the literary canon, argues that "Departments of literature in higher education, then, are part of the ideological state apparatus of the modern capitalist state".

The Safe Schools LGBTQI program, where gender is defined as fluid and limitless and children are taught that being male or female enforces a binary code that is heteronormative, represents an example of how literature is now being deconstructed and critiqued by the cultural-left.

Shakespeare's *Romeo and Juliet* is guilty of privileging heterosexuality, fairy tales like *Cinderella* are attacked for defining a happy ending as marrying the Prince, and children's books like Enid Blyton's *The Faraway Tree* for not portraying girls as dominant and in control.

As detailed by Gary Marks from the Australian Catholic University cultural-left theories like postmodernism are based on the belief that language and texts, whether literary or not, have no inherent meaning as they are simply instruments employed by ruling class elites to enforce domination and control.

Supposedly, Western, liberal democracies are riven with inequality and injustice and, as a result Marks writes, "postmodernism assumes that these inequalities are extreme and unchanging and it is the task of postmodernism to expose how these inequities are maintained by deconstructing language and text".

Deconstructionism and postmodernism also deny the referential quality of language and lead to the situation where it is impossible to argue that the author exists or that his or her works can have an agreed meaning.

A situation, as described by the Australian academic Brian Crittenden, where "… the author (writer or speaker) does not exist — or, at least, has no privileged position on the question of what he or she meant by a particular use of language. The text (in whatever form it comes) is open to unlimited possibilities of interpretation (or deconstruction)".

In opposition to the cultural-left's rainbow alliance of theories that now dominate the academy it is vital to acknowledge and celebrate the strengths of a liberal education. The argument that all knowledge is a socio-cultural construct based on power and privilege and that texts have no agreed meaning is contradictory and self-defeating.

The belief that truth is relative or simply the result of power relationships makes it impossible to objectively identify what is true and what is false or what more closely approximates reality. A commitment to rationality and empiricism only works when there is agreement about what constitutes what is right and what is wrong.

To equate education with indoctrination and imposing a politically correct ideology on students is also misplaced.

A liberal education, on the other hand, is based on the pursuit of truth and the need for an open and free dialogue where often conflicting ideas and concepts are allowed to be voiced.

A liberal education, in addition to being impartial and balanced, is also one that is inherently moral and that draws on the established disciplines that can be traced back via the Reformation, the Enlightenment and Renaissance to ancient Rome and Greece.

As noted by Matthew Arnold, while acknowledging and respecting the past, a liberal education is one that evolves and changes as it is committed to turning "a stream of fresh and free thought upon our stock notions and habits which we now follow staunchly but mechanically".

Wear it Purple Day and other cultural-left moves sending us puce

Given the re-emergence of the Safe Schools program, the NSW primary school putting on a stolen generation play where children dress as nuns and victimise aboriginal children and the Australian Education Union's campaign to promote the LGBTQI 'Wear it Purple Day' there's no doubt that the cultural-left now dominates our education system.

For the overwhelming majority of parents, the reason they send their children to school is to learn the basics, to socialise with other students and to acquire the knowledge and skills to be good citizens and to be better prepared for further study or the workforce.

Not so according to the cultural-left's Australian Education Union and like-minded bureaucrats and academics that are using the education system and schools to radically reshape society by indoctrinating students with Marxist inspired, politically correct ideologies.

The Safe Schools program indoctrinates children with the belief that gender and sexuality are fluid and limitless and Roz Ward, who helped design the program, argues, "it will only be through a revitalised class struggle and revolutionary change that we can hope for the liberation of LGBTI people".

Like the Safe Schools program those organising the 'Wear it Purple Day' are committed to "Ensuring diverse expressions of sex, sexuality and gender" and it should not surprise that the organisers actively support the Sydney Gay & Lesbian Mardi Gras.

Friday 25th August is 'Wear it Purple Day' and the New South Wales Teachers Federation is telling schools they should link "the key ideas of Wear It Purple Day to broader lessons on diversity and difference, to foster safe and supportive environments. The event embraces and celebrates sexuality, sex and gender diversity".

Further evidence of the Australian Education Union's politically correct ideology is its response to the postal same-sex marriage plebiscite. The President of the AEU Ms Haythorpe argues "The AEU is strongly opposed to the Federal government's approach, which is more about satisfying the bigotry of sections of the Liberal Party, rather than the interests or will of the community".

Like so many of the cultural-left elites dominating the public and political debate the Australian Education Union and Ms Haythorpe believe anyone who disagrees is a bigot and that the people, instead of expressing their views and opinions as is their democratic right, must be silenced.

And it's been happening for years. In 1983 Joan Kirner, the one-time Victorian education minister and premier, argued at a Fabian Society conference that education "has to be part of the socialist struggle for equality, participation and social change rather than an instrument of the capitalist system".

The AEU's 2003 'Policy on Gay, Lesbian, Bisexual and Transgender People' adopted by the teacher union argues "Sexuality should be included in all curriculum relating to health and personal development. Homosexuality and bisexuality need to be normalised and materials need to be developed which will help to combat homophobia".

As noted, the Australian Education Union has a long history of cultural-left political activism and promoting left-wing causes like same sex-marriage, gender fluidity and a secular curriculum that undermines the value of Western culture by promoting diversity and difference — the new code for multiculturalism.

Since the late '70s and early '80s the left-wing teacher union has argued that Australian society is riven with inequality and injustice and that the school curriculum must be used to promote its politically correct views about global warming, the evils of capitalism, that men are misogynist and sexist and that there's nothing beneficial about meritocracy and competition.

Such is the success of the Australian Education Union to take control of the school curriculum that a past president of the union argues "we have succeeded in influencing curriculum development in schools, education departments and universities. The conservatives have a lot to do to undo the progressive curriculum".

Examples of the cultural-left's takeover of the curriculum include the fact that students are now taught that gender and sexuality are "social constructions" that promote "unequal power relationships" between boys and girls and that those who believe in traditional marriage are guilty of "heteronormativity".

While the Australian Education Union and like-minded academics argue against schools teaching about Christianity or having formal religious instruction classes they are happy to pressure schools to worship the Gaia by including Al Gore's DVDs in the curriculum.

There is an alternative to Marxist inspired indoctrination if politicians and education bureaucrats have the courage to act. Education should never be confused with indoctrination and the curriculum must be impartial and balanced.

The school curriculum should also teach students the importance of civility, humility and a commitment to being rational, honest and ethical in their behaviour and relationships with others.

Students must be taught the strengths and benefits of Western civilisation, as well as the flaws and weaknesses, and that to be fully and properly educated they need to be familiar with what the Victorian Blackburn Report describes as "our best validated knowledge and artistic achievements".

Undermined from within

There's no doubt that Western cultures, especially those associated with the Anglosphere (including the United Kingdom, Australia, New Zealand, America and Canada) are bastions of freedom, democracy, high standards of living and scientific progress and innovation.

And it's clear what makes Western culture unique. Compared to military dictatorships and oppressive regimes across Asia, the Middle East and parts of South America and Africa, Western nations share variations of a Westminster style of parliamentary democracy and a political system committed to 'life, liberty and the pursuit of happiness'.

We also share a legal system the guarantees the right to a fair trial, innocence until proven guilty and the right to be judged by one's peers. Add Christian inspired values like sanctity of life, free will and a commitment to social justice and the common good and it's clear why so many millions of refugees are flooding to the West.

Best illustrated by the Enlightenment Western culture also has developed a unique approach to science based on rationality and reason. Instead of superstition, witchcraft or hearsay Western science is based on logic and what can be proven to be true or false.

It should not surprise that all of the most influential breakthroughs and developments in medicine, science and technology since the industrial revolution have occurred in Western nations.

Proven by the example of Sydney's Campion College Western culture has also developed a unique approach to education that also explains why we are so successful. The purpose of education, instead of being utilitarian or promoting self-interest, is committed to knowledge, wisdom and truth.

Cardinal Newman's ideal of a university education is one that is "disciplined for its own sake, for the perception of its higher object, and for its highest culture". While professional qualifications are important a broad education including disciplines like history, literature, music, art and languages are vital if one is to be truly educated.

Notwithstanding the strengths and benefits of Western culture since the late '60s it has been attacked by both enemies foreign and domestic. Islamic fundamentalism represents a physical threat where groups like ISIS use terrorism to create a climate of fear.

Examples include the 9/11 attack on the US and the death and destruction in London, Manchester, Paris, Nice as well as Sydney and Melbourne. Add the Bali bombings and it's clear, as argued by Ayaan Hirsi Ali, that "Islam is not a religion of peace".

While the vast majority of Muslims around the world and in Australia peacefully co-exist, the reality is that the Koran justifies a fatwa against the West, especially Christians, and that in countries like Saudi Arabia and Iran citizens, especially women, are denied the rights we take for granted

Unlike Christianity that allows disagreement when interpreting the Bible, it's also the case that Muslim preachers believe the Koran must be taken literally and that those who question its legitimacy are guilty of apostasy and must be condemned.

At the same time Western nations are being attacked by Islamic terrorists our way of life is also being undermined from within. Since the late '60s cultural-left radicals have taken 'the long march' through institutions like schools, universities, the public service and the media to impose their revolutionary, politically correct agenda.

Victoria's one-time education minister, Joan Kirner, argued that education had to be part of the "socialist struggle for equality, participation and social change, rather than an instrument of the capitalist system".

Supposedly, our education system reinforces conservative values and Western culture is oppressive, misogynist, racist and guilty of enforcing inequality. In schools Marxist LGBTQI gender theory is forced on students and the national curriculum ignores Western culture in favour of politically correct indigenous, Asian and sustainability perspectives.

Proven by the Institute of Public Affairs analysis it is also true that "undergraduate history degrees in Australia fail to teach fundamental aspects of Australian history (instead) focusing on popular culture, film studies and ethnic/ race history".

According to one academic at Sydney University teaching the benefits of Western culture is wrong because it "replicates and reinforces the concept of whiteness". A situation leading to "racism, sexism, classism, historical injustice and prejudice based on religion".

Thought police screening schoolbooks

Victoria's politically correct thought police and nanny state mentality know no bounds. The Marxist-inspired LGBTQI gender and sexuality program is being forced on all government schools, as is the Respectful Relationships program that presents boys and men as violent and misogynist.

Add the state's Curriculum and Assessment Authority's principles and guidelines dictating what texts should be studied in years 11 and 12, and it's no wonder Victoria is once again being described as our Albania of the South — a state where cultural-left ideology and group-think rules, and freedom of thought is under threat.

The guidelines warn that texts should not be chosen "regardless of literary or dramatic merit" if they deal with "violence or physical, psychological or sexual abuse", "gratuitous use of coarse language" or they "promote or normalise the abuse of alcohol, the use of illegal drugs or other illegal behaviour".

Texts dealing with the full ambit of human nature with all its flaws, weaknesses and susceptibility to give in to temptation are to be cut from the state-mandated curriculum.

Often the most enduring and worthwhile examples of literature by their very nature portray the dark and unsettling side of humanity and personal relationships. In the Greek tragedy *The Bacchae*, Euripides presents Dionysus as a god of wine, promiscuity and physical gratification that represents an enduring aspect of human nature.

Other Greek tragedies, such as *Antigone* and *King Oedipus*, centre on the nature and impact of violence, deceit, betrayal and the impact of psychological and sexual abuse.

Shakespeare's *Macbeth*, as vividly portrayed in Roman Polanski's film adaptation, is awash with violence and death, and there's no escaping the reality that what drives Lady Macbeth to suicide is her mental and psychological instability.

The final scene of *Hamlet* is also bloody, and once again the destructive impact of psychological abuse is evident with Ophelia's suicide.

As proved by one of Shakespeare's most memorable characters, Falstaff, it's also true that great literature often involves bawdy scenes involving alcohol and rude and offensive language.

Similar to Falstaff, the central character in *Zorba the Greek* would fall foul of today's PC thought police as he is consumed by the attraction of women and drink, illustrated by his statement: "To be alive is to undo your belt and look for trouble."

There's also no doubt that if the Victorian guidelines relating to "social and sexual relationships" are taken seriously then metaphysical poets like Marvell and Donne would be unacceptable.

Marvell's *To His Coy Mistress* is a seduction poem feminists would castigate as misogynist in nature as the poet's aim is to convince his mistress to consummate their relationship "like amorous birds of prey". Donne's poem *Elegie: To his Mistress Going to Bed* would also definitely be in the no-go zone as the lines, "Licence my roving hands, and let them go, Behind, before, above, between, below", would cause feminist apoplexy.

Modern Australian classics like *Wake in Fright, The One Day of the Year* and *Don's Party*, given the pervasive influence of alcohol, gambling and sexual innuendo and misbehaviour, would also fall foul of the politically correct mentality that seeks to impose state sanctioned behaviour.

And what of Tolstoy's *War and Peace*, that vast and majestic novel that not only vividly and in detail portrays the death, suffering and violence of war but also the interplay of characters depicting the full range of human emotions and actions including sexual promiscuity, betrayal and abuse?

Whatever the nature of the text or how challenging its issues, teachers must ensure the way it is taught is affirmative and constructive, that lessons include a range of perspectives and there are alternative points of view.

DH Lawrence argues: "The Business of art is to reveal the relation between man and his circumambient universe at the living moment." Lawrence also argues that literature should never be sanitised and, as such, students have the right to encounter human nature and their world in all its complexity and challenges — good and evil, dark and light.

Twisting the tale to suit cultural-left's agenda

Nothing is safe when it comes to the cultural-left's campaign to force identity politics on the public in its quest to radically reshape society. Identity politics involves positively discriminating in favour of minority groups and demonising the vast majority of people who are normal.

And identity politics is a key strategy in the cultural-left's long march through institutions like the family, schools, universities and churches in its attempt to create a socialist, politically correct utopia.

As Hollywood is a seedbed for the cultural-left it should not surprise that the latest example of identity politics involves Disney's interpretation of the classic children's story, *Beauty and the Beast*, where Gaston's sidekick LeFou is portrayed as gay.

In an interview published in the UK's gay magazine *Attitude*, the film's director Bill Condon describes LeFou as "somebody who on one day wants to be Gaston and, on another day, wants to kiss Gaston".

The director describes one scene in the film as an "exclusively gay moment" and Josh Gad, who acts the part of LeFou, describes portraying Disney's first ever LGBTQI character as "incredible".

Ignored is that the original story and earlier adaptations celebrated love between a woman and a prince without any reference to a gay relationship.

And rewriting *Beauty and the Beast* is just the most recent example of the cultural-left's campaign against classic fairy tales and stories and indoctrinating children with its view of what is politically correct.

Little Black Sambo has been removed from school libraries, supposedly, as it presents a demeaning caricature of 'people of colour'. *Thomas the Tank Engine*, according to a Marxist interpretation, reinforces inequality because bus and freight trains are inferior to main line trains and the Fat Controller dominates all.

Feminists argue that stories like *Cinderella*, where the happy ending involves Cinderella marrying the handsome prince, are unacceptable as they privilege heterosexual love. Apparently, it's wrong for children to believe that gender and sexuality are binary where men and women form a natural partnership.

Enid Blyton's series of books *The Faraway Tree* are also guilty as it's the boys who are assertive and in control. In Victoria, a primary school changed the lyrics to *Kookaburra sits on the old gum tree* by erasing the description 'gay' as it might offend homosexuals.

Traditional tales, in the words of one Australian academic, reinforce "phallus-dominated heterosexuality and female dependence". Politically correct gender theory teaches it is wrong to portray men as masculine and to depict women as wives and mothers.

Another academic describes the English classroom as a socio-political site where classic fables and stories impose an "oppressive male-female dualistic hierarchy" and a "phallogo-centric signifying system for making meaning".

Put simply, notwithstanding that approximately 98% of Australians identify as being male or female, the cultural-left argues that plays like *Romeo and Juliet* unfairly reinforce heterosexuality as the norm.

While most parents would dismiss such arguments as politically correct mumbo-jumbo the reality is that identity politics, especially the LGBTQI agenda, now dominates the education system.

Schools across Australia celebrate the national 'Wear it Purple' campaign and the LGBTQI film *Gayby Baby* suggests there is nothing special or unique about marriage involving a man or a woman — instead marriage can involve a man and a man or a woman and a woman.

In the children's story, *The Gender Fairy*, primary school children are told that gender is fluid and limitless and that "only you know whether you are a boy or a girl. No one can tell you".

The Safe Schools LGBTQI program, under the pretence of being an anti-bullying program, indoctrinates children with the belief that 10% of young people are same-sex attracted even though the correct figure is more like 1 to 2%.

One of the resources published by the La Trobe University's Research Centre in Sex, Health and Society, titled *Freedom Fighters*, gets students to sing "you don't have to be a certain way just because you have a penis, you don't have to be a certain way just because you have a vagina".

Identity politics also means the school curriculum forces multiculturalism on students even though we are a Christian nation where parliaments begin with the Lord's Prayer and 61% of Australians identify as Christian with Islam at 2.2%, Hinduism 1.3% and Buddhism at 2.4%.

Instead of celebrating and defending Western culture the cultural-left champions cultural relativism where anyone who defends our way of life is attacked as Islamophobic, racist and a deplorable.

Left's war on the West

There's no doubt that the culture wars are escalating and that the election campaign is turning out to be a battleground between the cultural-left, represented by the Greens and the ALP, and the Coalition government.

The Greens Party's policy is to fully fund the radical LGBTQI Safe Schools Coalition program that indoctrinates children as young as four and five with its message that there is nothing natural or beneficial about the love between a man and women.

Gender is fluid and limitless and because it is a social construct boys can be girls and girls can be boys in this dystopian brave new world of the future.

And it now appears that the ALP federal opposition will follow the Greens and the socialist-left Victorian Andrews government — that refuses to modify the program in response to the commonwealth review — and fully support the program.

It's also true that both the Greens and the ALP support same-sex marriage on the basis that there is nothing natural or beneficial in marriage involving a man and women for the purpose of procreation.

Add the fact that the Greens want to abolish the exemptions faith-based schools and organisations have to discriminate in who they employ or who they do business with and it's clear that the battle lines are being drawn.

And there is also no doubt that those opposed to radical change are in danger of losing the battle of ideas and what ex-Prime Minister Julia Gillard once described as the culture wars.

The political correctness movement is alive and well in our universities where students are told Australia was invaded and that today's white Australians must feel guilty about what happened over 200 years ago.

While we once laughed at slogans like 'land rights for gay whales' anybody who now steps out of line is censored by the cultural-left thought-police and made to recant.

While the Catholic Church is attacked for writing to companies like Telstra expressing its concern about business groups publicly supporting same-sex marriage, the left activists feel free to condemn and boycott superannuation industries that invest in coal.

The Australian National Curriculum airbrushes Christianity from history and civics and Western civilisation is ignored in favour of cultural relativism and uncritically celebrating diversity and difference — the new code for multiculturalism.

In explaining why the cultural-left has been so successful it is important to go back to the late '60s — the time of Vietnam moratoriums, the counter-culture movement, the birth control pill and books like Germaine Greer's *The Female Eunuch*.

Across the Western world, especially in France, America and Australia, university students and academics rebelled against traditional authority represented by the family, the Church, schools and the state.

Based on European Marxist philosophers and sociologists like Antonio Gramsci, Louis Althusser and Pierre Bourdieu the cultural-left argued that Western societies are riven with inequality and injustice and the only way forward is to take the long march through the institutions.

On American campuses radical students chanted "Hey, hey, ho, ho, Western Civ has got to go" and in Australian universities students held sit-ins and argued that subjects like history and literature have no inherent value as they reproduce the power of the dominant class.

Victimhood became the order of the day and the cultural-left enforced a politically correct agenda based on the new trinity of 'gender, ethnicity and class'.

In Victoria the one-time education minister, Joan Kirner, argued at a Fabian Society meeting that schools had to become "part of the socialist struggle for equality, participation and social change, rather than an instrument of the capitalist system".

Two American academics popular at the same time argued that schools must become the front line for radical change on the basis that "Inequalities in education are part of the web of capitalist society and are likely to persist as long as capitalism survives".

Teacher unions like the NSW Teachers Federation argued in a similar fashion when stating that the school curriculum must take into account "The role of the economy, the sexual division of labour, the dominant culture and education systems in reproducing inequality".

Forget Mark Latham's belief that education provided a ladder of opportunity and that so many disadvantaged students have overcome poverty because Australia is an egalitarian society where all, with ability and motivation, can succeed.

The Australian Association for the Teaching of English also adopted a cultural-left ideology. The AATE's journal, after the election of the Howard Government in 2004, argued that teachers had failed to teach "critical literacy" because so many voters preferred a conservative government.

Examples like the Victorian Government removing Religious Instruction from the school timetable and forcing schools to embrace a PC ideology in areas like the environment and Indigenous history proves how successful the cultural-left's long march has been.

The fact that approximately 800 Australian businesses and corporations can go public endorsing same-sex marriage while the Catholic Bishops are attacked for putting the counter-case in the *Don't Mess With Marriage* booklet also illustrates how dire the situation is.

Whitewashing history makes fools of us all

The story about the University of NSW Diversity Toolkit telling
academics and students that Australia was "invaded" and it
is wrong to suggest Captain Cook discovered Australia or to
describe pre-European indigenous culture as "primitive" should
not surprise.

The toolkit, available on the university's website and based
on one developed at Flinders University, confirms the fact many
of our universities are now controlled by the politically correct
thought police of the cultural-left.

The toolkit details the process to be followed to ensure
that what is taught and how students learn embraces "Cultural
Diversity and Inclusive Practice (CDIP)".

Forget about basing learning on what is objective, scien-
tifically proven or pursuing wisdom and truth regardless of
cultural diversity and difference.

Under the headings Culturally Inclusive Environment,
Culturally Inclusive Practice and Appropriate Terminology,
indigenous Australian People, lecturers and tutors are warned
about what constitutes acceptable and unacceptable behaviour.

Also forget about free speech and open inquiry. Academics
are told that the guidelines "explicitly state the need to embrace
different cultures and accommodate diverse educational back-
grounds in the student body".

On the assumption that Australia is truly multicultural, academics are also told they must "acknowledge, value and draw
on the diversity of students' experiences in teaching activities".

The toolkit goes on to say: "Students and staff can benefit
from culturally inclusive practice and experience diversity as a
resource that enriches our teaching, learning, research, service

provision and other work." Except if you are white and of Anglo-Celtic descent where academics are warned: "Students who see themselves as part of the dominant culture are likely to be resistant to course material that questions existing power relations and privilege."

The implication is students identified as part of the dominant culture need to be re-educated in terms of what is politically correct. Like trigger warnings on US campuses, where minority students are warned about material they might find offensive, the CDIP Toolkit tells academics they must "include statements about processes and expectations for discussing controversial material".

Ignored is that the true purpose of a university education, as argued by Cardinal Newman so many years ago, is to pursue wisdom, knowledge and truth regardless of cultural background or ideological bias.

Also ignored is the concept of a university and a liberal education is culturally specific and no amount of jargon about respecting diversity can deny that Western civilisation is the birthplace of our education system.

The University of NSW toolkit is an example of how the cultural-left's long march through our universities has been so successful. In 1996, such was the destructive impact of the political correctness movement that Pierre Ryckmans in his ABC Boyer Lecture concluded that "the university as Western civilisation knew it is now virtually dead".

In 2008 a group of students were so concerned about being force-fed cultural-left ideology they organised a conference in Sydney titled Silencing Dissent. Example after example was given of students, in subjects such as history, literature, sociology and the law being criticised for arguing from a conservative perspective and daring to question the cultural-left orthodoxy.

In literature, authors and playwrights such as Anthony Trollope, Charles Dickens and Shakespeare were criticised as dead, white, European males (DWEMS) and students were made to deconstruct texts in terms of power relationships and the hegemony of the ruling class.

Students had to accept that cultural relativism prevailed and it was wrong to discriminate or favour one culture over another.

The University of NSW Diversity Toolkit represents the natural outcome of the cultural-left's long march through the institutions, especially of higher learning.

In history, Western civilisation was characterised as racist, imperialistic and capitalist by nature and anyone who defended it was attacked as Eurocentric, patriarchal and ethnically challenged.

Children's schooling suffers as teachers pursue Marxist agenda

There's nothing new in NSW's Helensburgh Public School using Year 3 children as refugee activists and classroom teachers wearing T-shirts with the slogan "Teachers for Refugees — Close the Camps, Bring Them Here".

The NSW Teachers Federation and the Australian Education Union have a long history of using the education system to indoctrinate students with Marxist-inspired causes.

In 2002, after the Howard government committed troops to Iraq, the AEU directed teachers to "take action in your workplace and community" and to "support students who take an anti-war stance (and to) encourage participation in peaceful protests".

Instead of education and the curriculum being objective, whereby students are taught to be critical-minded and to weigh alternative points of view, the AEU's leadership is only concerned with imposing its politically correct views on controversial issues. While parents are shocked by the Marxist-inspired Safe Schools LGBTQI program, which teaches children gender is fluid and celebrating being a man or a woman is heteronormative, the AEU gives it full support. Its federal president, Correna Haythorpe, describes critics of the Safe Schools program as "extreme conservatives" opposing a "highly effective and positive program".

At a time when Australia's international test results are in free fall, the AEU, instead of focusing on the basics, is more interested in campaigning for "global movements for peace, social justice, nuclear disarmament, justice for refugees and the environment".

In relation to climate change, AEU Victorian branch president Meredith Peace is happy to visit schools as a result of being trained "by Al Gore to give his famous climate change presentation as part of his Climate Project".

Since its establishment in the early 1990s, the AEU and its state and territory branches have campaigned for a plethora of neo-Marxist, feminist, LGBTQI and postcolonial causes. Such is the success of the AEU in determining what happens in the school curriculum that a past president, Pat Byrne, was able to boast "the conservatives have a lot of work to do to undo the progressive curriculum".

Instead of celebrating Australia's economic successes, our high standard of living and the fact that we are a peaceful, democratic nation, the AEU argues the curriculum must critique the "role of the economy, the sexual division of labour, the dominant culture and the education system in reproducing inequality".

As such, the AEU is a long-time critic of the academic curriculum and meritocracy, where there are winners and losers.

Supposedly, based on a Marxist view of society, the traditional curriculum and competition reinforce capitalist hegemony and the power of the ruling class.

Instead of ranking students in terms of motivation and ability, and holding schools responsible for results, the AEU argues learning must "be premised on co-operation rather than competition and the prospect of success rather than failure".

Drawing on communist theorists such as Antonio Gramsci, Pierre Bourdieu and Louis Althusser, schools are condemned as essential parts of the ideological state apparatus that, as a result, must by captured and transformed.

As prominent Victorian union activist Bill Hannan argued some years ago, "We don't have to wait for society to change before education can change. Education is part of society. By changing it, we help to change society."

Or, as argued by the then left-wing Victorian education minister Joan Kirner, "we have to reshape education so that it is part of the socialist struggle for equality, participation and social change, rather than instrument of the capitalist system".

Not surprisingly, given its old-style statist view of education, where governments, bureaucracies and teacher unions enforce a command-and-control model of public policy, the AEU opposes the existence and funding of Catholic and independent schools.

Even though parents are voting with their feet and about 35% of students attend non-government schools, the AEU argues "there is no pre-existing, predetermined entitlement to public funding: i.e. there is no a priori justification for public funding to private schools".

By denying funding to non-government schools and arguing that additional billions must be spent on government schools, especially to employ more teachers and prospective union members, the AEU is obviously driven by self-interest.

Self-interest also explains why the AEU is committed to an antiquated and inflexible centralised enterprise bargaining system, one that ensures its seat at the table and that denies individual schools the freedom to shape employment conditions that best suit local needs.

Ignored is the international movement to free schools from provider capture, represented by charter schools in the US and free schools in England, and to give them the autonomy to best meet the needs and aspirations of their local communities.

Instead of educating students in a balanced and impartial way the AEU is committed to indoctrinating children with neo-Marxist, politically correct groupthink.

The West's foes, foreign and domestic

What makes Western culture unique and is it worthwhile defending? Given events, both foreign and domestic, the question is a vital one as the answer will determine whether countries like Australia survive and prosper or whether, as we currently know them, they cease to exist.

T. S. Eliot in *Notes Towards a Definition of Culture* defines culture as "a way of life of a particular people living together in one place" and includes a people's social system, habits, customs and, most importantly, religion.

In his 1996 Boyer Lecture, the Australian academic Pierre Ryckmans describes culture "as the true and unique signature of man" and in the same way a garden is cultivated it is vital that society cultivates the young to enable them to preserve and enrich the culture in which they are born.

Based on the example of China, Ryckmans goes on to argue it is impossible to understand a foreign culture unless you have a "firm grasp of your own culture" and, as a result, "the luxury which no country can ever afford, in any circumstances... is to dispense with its memory and its imagination".

One only has to study history or be aware of current events around the world to appreciate that cultures rise and fall and that Western culture, in particular, is under attack by enemies both foreign and domestic.

The violence and terror associated with Islamic fundamentalism illustrated by attacks in London, Paris, Nice, New York, Boston, Melbourne and Sydney represent an external threat that strikes at the heart of our way of life.

Indiscriminate and random acts where innocents are killed and maimed, in addition to creating an atmosphere of intimidation and fear, lead to governments introducing security laws that are in danger of compromising the freedoms and rights so often taken for granted.

As noted by the Somalian activist Ayaan Hirsi Ali in her book *Heretic*, Islam is not a religion of peace and terrorist groups like ISIS, in addition to waging violent jihad against the West, are committed to establishing an Islamic caliphate where non-believers face conversion, subjugation or death.

The mass migration of Muslims from the Middle East and Northern Africa to England and Europe also represents a clear and present danger to the liberties and freedoms central to the West's way of life.

Whether Islamic youth rioting in the suburbs of Paris, German women being physically and sexually accosted in Cologne and Hamburg during New Year, the incidence of female genital mutilation in England or the ever-increasing incidence of rape in Sweden by Islamic men the reality is our way of life is under threat.

As well as the enemy without, Western culture is also facing the enemy within. Instead of acknowledging the strengths and benefits of Western culture dating back to ancient Greece and Rome the cultural-left condemns the West as Eurocentric, misogynist, imperialistic and self-serving.

As the result of a rainbow alliance of cultural-left theories, including poststructuralism, deconstruction, post-colonialism, neo-Marxism, feminism and LGBTQI gender theory our universities are no longer committed to objectivity and the dis-interested pursuit of knowledge, wisdom and truth.

Feminists argues that the Western concept of rationality is a binary, phallocentric construct employed to dominate and subjugate women. Deconstructionists argue that it is impossible to agree on the referential quality of words and that meaning is both subjective and relative. Post-colonialism, instead of accepting there might be something worthwhile about Western culture, sees it as simply concerned with the subjugation and exploitation of the third world.

Such is the parlous and fraught nature of scholastic endeavour that Pierre Ryckmans in his 1996 lecture argues that "to deny the existence of objective values is to deprive the uni-versity of its spiritual means of operation".

The Melbourne based academic John Carroll writes, "(the Left's) carping negativity continues to thrive. Using neo-Marxist categories of exploitation and oppression to find "victims" of their own country's mendacity, as a device to whip it — so Australia becomes racist, cruel to refugees, misogynist, homophobic and increasingly riven by inequality. The tropes endure, with Islam the current exploited and oppressed repository of virtue".

And the school curriculum is also being subverted by the cultural-left. As noted by the National Curriculum Review that I co-chaired, whether history, civics, art, literature or music, the contribution made by Western culture is ignored in favour of indoctrinating students with the politically correct trinity of indigenous, Asian and environmental cross-curriculum priorities.

Many on the cultural-left also argue that there is nothing superior or preferable about Western science as it is only one science among many and cannot be considered privileged. Western science and technology, instead of improving the health and wellbeing of millions across the globe, are condemned for polluting and destroying the planet.

Ignored are the millions in the third world that are healthier and better fed because of advances in agriculture and public health as a result of innovations and discoveries brought about by Western science, technology and medicine.

The International Food Policy Research Institute measures global hunger according to the proportion of people who are undernourished, the proportion of children under 5 who are underweight and the mortality rate of children under 5 (termed the Global Hunger Index or GHI). Instead of doom and gloom the Institute reports:

"Compared to the 1990 GHI score, the 2014 GHI score is 28 percent lower in Africa south of the Sahara, 41 percent lower in South Asia, and 40 percent lower in the Middle East and North Africa. The score for East and Southeast Asia fell by 54 percent and Latin America and the Caribbean saw a drop of 53 percent".

While many on the cultural-left argue that Western culture is oppressive and that victim groups like women, migrants, working class and LGBTQI people are denied equity and social justice, as proven by an analysis undertaken by the American-based Freedom House, the opposite is the case.

In our own region, while Australia and New Zealand are given the highest ratings for protecting civil liberties and political rights countries like China, Thailand, Myanmar, Lao PDR, Vietnam and Cambodia are given a lower rating and are categorised as least free.

What the American Declaration of Independence describes as the right to enjoy "life, liberty and the pursuit of happiness" has not happened by accident and is unique to Western culture. Liberty, equality, freedom of speech, the right to vote, innocent until proven guilty, the right to a fair trial and the right to own property and to make a profit can only be understood and valued in the context of Western culture.

Beginning with the ancient Greeks and the concept of demos and evolving over hundreds of years and including Magna Carta, the Westminster form of government and common law and the Enlightenment those lucky enough to live in Western cultures enjoy unparalleled freedoms.

In what is an increasingly secular age, it is also important to recognise the historical and on-going significance of Christianity, especially the Catholic Church. As detailed by Larry Siedentop in *Inventing the Individual: The Origins of Western Liberalism* Christian concepts like the sanctity of life, free will and all being equal in the eyes of God underpin Western legal and political systems.

The Perth-based academic Augusto Zimmermann also argues that Christianity has had a significant influence on our legal system when he writes:

"It can, at the very least, be said that Judeo-Christian values were so embedded in Australia so as to necessitate the recognition of God in the nation's founding document. When considered alongside the development of colonial laws, the adoption of the English common-law tradition and American system of federation, it is evident that the foundations of the Australian nation, and its laws, have discernible Christian-philosophical roots".

While ignored by the Australian National Curriculum, it is also true that to study music, art, literature or architecture without a knowledge and appreciation of Christianity is to be culturally impoverished. Whether Chaucer's Canterbury Tales, Dante's Inferno, Bach's Mass in B Minor, Vivaldi's Requiem, Michelangelo's Pietta or the Sistine Chapel the reality is that Christianity has had, and continues to have, a profound impact.

Like the air we breathe, we are surrounded and immersed in Western culture and the danger is, like oxygen, once we discover it is no longer there it is too late.

Culture wars: the left's university loonies

The culture wars are fought on two fronts. The first involves Islamic State and its jihad against Western civilisation, illustrated by the Paris terrorist attacks, the beheading of 21 Christians in Libya, the London bombings and the Lindt Cafe siege.

The second front involves the clash between those defending Western culture, including our Judaeo-Christian heritage and secular humanism, and those cultural-left critics who argue that Western cultures such as Australia are Eurocentric, discriminatory and guilty of reinforcing disadvantage.

The University of Sydney's Religion State and Society Research Network best illustrates how those from the cultural-left are seeking to attack and undermine Western culture.

Any curriculum that defends Western political and legal systems and way of life is attacked on the network's website for replicating and reinforcing what is described as "the socially constructed concept of whiteness".

The Sydney University network goes on to argue that the "dominance of whiteness in the curriculum" represents "an ideology of power" that is guilty of "advancing Eurocentric notions as neutral and normal".

Supposedly, values and beliefs that make Western culture unique, such as individual liberty, freedom of expression, sanctity of life and the right to vote, are simply social constructs that promote "exclusion, implicit bias, structural inequality and intersectional discrimination".

Based on this argument the reason so many hundreds of young men from Britain and Australia have joined IS is because they are victims of an unfair and unjust society where they feel unwanted and excluded.

The network, in part funded by the Australian and Malaysia Institute and Council of Australian Arab Relations and associated with Muslim-majority states and the Muslim diaspora, calls on Australian universities "to dismantle the white curriculum" and to "criticise the reproduction of whiteness".

The irony, of course, is that the only reason groups such as Sydney University's Religion State and Society Research Network are allowed to criticise Western values and institutions is because of the very freedoms and liberties that make our culture unique.

A Saudi Arabian court sentenced the poet Ashraf Fayadh to death for being an atheist and, supposedly, for criticising the Prophet Mohammed. Somali-born activist Ayaan Hirsi Ali is under 24-hour protection after a fatwa was decreed against her for criticising aspects of the Islamic religion.

And in Islamic states such as Iran, where there is strict censorship and government control over the media, it is common for religious police to enforce sharia law by denying basic civil liberties and freedoms that we, in Australia, take for granted.

The re-emergence of the political correctness movement on university and college campuses in Australia, America and Britain provides further examples of the cultural-left's antipathy to Western culture and its tendency to rewrite history.

Student activists at Oxford University's Oriel College are running a campaign vilifying the British colonial mining magnate and businessman Cecil Rhodes. As it happens, one of the leading campaigners against Rhodes, South African Ntokozo Qwabe, is a Rhodes scholar.

The decision by the University of Texas to remove the statue of Jefferson Davis, the first and only president of the Confederate states during the American Civil War, is also being criticised for giving in to the political correctness movement.

While there is no doubt that Davis, like the Confederate flag, offends many Americans because of an association with slavery, the reality is that removing his statue, as if Davis never existed, denies the reality of past events.

Melbourne University is also experiencing its own version of sanitising the past where there is a campaign to rename five buildings because they offend cultural-left sensitivities.

Sanitising history to make the past conform to today's politically correct standards is not only guilty of rewriting the past. The cultural-left is also hypocritical in that communist dictators and tyrants such as Ho Chi Minh and Che Guevara are always celebrated as liberators and freedom fighters without any reference to their crimes against humanity.

Western civilisation's wan defenders

Samuel P. Huntington, over twenty years ago in The Clash of Civilizations, argued, "The great divisions among humankind and the dominating source of conflict will be cultural".

How prescient he was is proven by the fact that Western civilisation and the culture it embodies and safeguards are under threat. Islamic terrorism, the impact of the culture wars and postmodernism, the rise of statism and the pervasive influence of celebrity culture and the new technologies, to name a few, are all conspiring to undermine certainties and absolutes that, until recently, have stood the test of time.

The violence, death and destruction associated with Islamic terrorism both overseas and on Australian soil not only represents a physical threat; the nihilistic and evil ideology underpinning terrorist acts like 9/11and the murder of 21 Christians by Islamic state threaten democratic values and beliefs, since Magna Carta, that have evolved to safeguard the peace and prosperity of English speaking nations.

Even worse, apologists for those seeking to destroy our way of life refuse to acknowledge the true nature of Islamic terrorism, preferring to blame Western culture, supposedly, for excluding and marginalizing disaffected groups whose only recourse is to turn to violence.

The cultural-left, instead of developing a strong and convincing narrative about the strengths and benefits of Western culture (what is worth fighting for) engage in a narrative of self-recrimination and self-doubt.

Whereas our universities and our schools were once committed to the pursuit of what Matthew Arnold in Culture and Anarchy describes as "the best which has been thought and said", given the impact of deconstruction and postmodernism, there are no longer any truths that we can hold in common or consider absolute.

The established disciplines of knowledge, instead of having any inherent meaning or worth, are simply socio-cultural constructs that enforce false consciousness and the hegemony of the ruling class.

The purpose of education is not to seek wisdom or truth but to reveal how all relationships are based on power and how capitalist societies enforce inequality and disadvantage.

Such is the ubiquitous and intrusive nature of celebrity culture that generations of young people measure success in terms of how popular they are on social networking sites like YouTube, Facebook, Twitter and Instagram.

The never-ending pursuit of material possessions and physical gratification promoted by the more extreme forms of consumer capitalism add to a superficial and self-centred view of life that, while promising much, delivers little of enduring or transcendent value.

Instead of success arising from hard work, ability and application, everyone is entitled to their 15 minutes of fame and their moment in the spotlight. Whereas the printed word requires effort and concentration, the digital age embodies an iconographic world of ever flickering, superficial and transient images and sounds.

The impact of these changes on Western culture is significant and profound. Whereas previous generations acknowledged and celebrated our unique way of life, the cultural-left argues that Western civilisation is simply one culture among many.

According to the Australian national curriculum, Australia is a multi-cultural, multi-faith society, characterised by diversity and difference. A society where there is no agreed definition of citizenship as:

Individuals may identify with multiple 'citizenships' at any one point in time and over a period of time. Citizenship means different things to people at different times and depending on personal perspectives, their social situation and where they live.

Cultural relativism dictates that the way of life associated with our Western heritage and traditions is no longer superior or preferable. If true, one wonders on what basis we can say 'no' to child brides, female circumcision and a theocratic form of government.

Many from the cultural-left argue that institutions like the family, the Church, the education system and our political and legal systems are misogynist, Eurocentric, patriarchal, elitist and, worst of all, Christian.

The Australian Education Union in its curriculum policy argues that Australian society and culture are riven with inequality and injustice and, as a result, the school curriculum must acknowledge:

> The pronounced inequality in the distribution of social, economic, cultural and political resources and power between social groups, which restricts the life development of many.

Instead of being resilient and capable of overcoming adversity, the high rates of suicide and mental depression and illness are symptomatic of a 'victim' mentality where the belief is that whatever goes wrong must be the fault of somebody else.

In this brave new world of political correctness rights take precedence over responsibilities, the prevailing ethos is one of entitlements and the nanny state now intrudes into our public and private lives in a way never dreamt of by Aldous Huxley when he wrote *Brave New World*.

Complicating matters further for those committed to defending and preserving Western civilisation and its cultural capital is the inability or unwillingness of many conservatives to fight the culture wars and to engage in what John Howard, when Prime Minister, described as the battle of ideas.

As noted by Edwin Dyga, in the October 2014 edition of *Quadrant*, such is influence of the cultural-left dominated media, educational institutions, entertainment industry and progressive political parties that it takes a brave person to swim against the tide and to question prevailing orthodoxies.

Dyga argues, such has been the cultural-left's success in taking the long march through the institutions, that the situation is one where:

… all discourse is saturated with "progressive" ideology and its assumptions, making authentic challenges to the zeitgeist impossible for fear of reprisal. Political defeat, being ostracised from "polite society", loss of career and reputation: these are the consequences any individual can expect to suffer to varying degrees for expressing views deemed heretical by contemporary liberal sensibilities.

What's to be done? Sun Tzu's aphorism "If you know yourself but not the enemy, for every victory gained you will also suffer a defeat" highlights the necessity of identifying and understanding what motivates the cultural-left in what ex-Prime Minister Julia Gillard describes in a 2003 speech as the "culture war".

While always couched in terms of equity and social justice and strengthening the common good, in an attempt to create a utopia on this earth, the reality is that the cultural-left's agenda is driven by the politics of pragmatism, envy and a thirst for power and control.

In its more extreme form, and so graphically portrayed in George Orwell's *Animal Farm*, the socialist ideal 'from each according to his ability, to each according to his need' eventually deteriorates into a cruel, violent and unjust world no different from that which has been overthrown.

The French Revolution's cry of 'liberty, equality and fraternity', as Edmund Burke predicted, was soon drowned out by the reign of terror and the sound of Madame Guillotine and the shouts of the assembled mob.

No amount of propaganda, misplaced ideology or double think can disguise the harsh and brutal reality of Stalin's gulag, Mao's famines that killed millions and Pol Pot's killing fields.

More recent strategies used by the cultural-left to exert power and control, while not as brutal or violent, are equally as dangerous and effective.

Group think and indoctrination, ignoring or banishing dissenting voices and taking control of the instruments of public and intellectual discourse are all employed to ensure compliance.

The philosophy is also a levelling down one that opposes meritocracy, fostering individual effort and restricting the power of government. Especially, in areas like education the belief is that rewarding ability, effort and application is elitist and guilty of reinforcing inequity and social injustice.

Arising from the counter culture movement of the mid-to-late '60s, the philosophy underpinning a cultural-left agenda is inherently hostile to rationality, objectivity and a transcendent sense of life; the very things that underpin Western culture.

While old style Marxists believe in an objective reality, more recent manifestations of cultural-left thought argue that how we perceive the world is subjective, that there are no truths that we hold in common and that the academy must be transformed into an engine of social critique and radical change.

In addition to knowing your adversary, it is equally important to know and appreciate what it is you believe in and what you are seeking to defend.

The cultural capital associated with Western civilisation, as suggested by Matthew Arnold, embodies "the best which has been thought and said in the world".

Culture, while also referring to a way of life, in its deepest and most profound sense deals with wisdom and truth and moral and spiritual values and beliefs. Such knowledge and understanding does not happen intuitively or by accident.

Over some hundreds of years Western culture has become codified into a range of academic disciplines and artistic and creative activities, both theoretical and practical. Western culture is also unique given the historical significance and on-going benefits of university and school education.

Each discipline and each activity address fundamental truths about the nature of reality, the purpose of life, what it means to be fulfilled, how to decide right from wrong, what constitutes the good life and how best to serve the common good.

As argued by George Weigal, in *The Cube and the Cathedral*, while practical and utilitarian, such a view of culture is transcendent in nature and to be valued for its own sake. It addresses:

… what men and women honor, cherish and worship; by what societies deem to be good and true and noble; by the expressions they give to those convictions in language, literature, and the arts; by what individuals and societies are willing to stake their lives on.

Instead of being ossified and backward looking this view of culture is also dynamic and subject to revision and change. As noted by Arnold, the intention is to turn "a stream of fresh and free thought upon our stock notions and habits, which we now follow staunchly but mechanically".

Christianity and the Bible are also central to Western culture. Christ's story and the lessons from the Bible, especially the New Testament, have had, and continue to have, a profound impact on our legal and political systems, ethics and philosophy, the arts, literature and our way of life.

Western culture is also variegated in nature and, while being unique, over some thousands of years has drawn on a range of other cultures and traditions in areas like science, mathematics, architecture, language, literature, music and the arts.

The Somalia activist, Ayaan Hirsi Ali, on being asked what can be done to counter Islamic terrorism argued that physical force was not enough.

To counter evil beliefs and indoctrination the West had to "inculcate into the minds and hearts of young people an ideology or ideas of life, love, peace and tolerance". The very attributes associated with Western civilisation that define our culture and that must be defended.

Turning the West into a wasteland

There is no doubt that Western civilisation and the culture it embodies and safeguards are under threat. Islamic terrorism, the impact of the culture wars and postmodernism, to name a few, are all conspiring to undermine certainties that have stood the test of time.

The violence, death and destruction associated with Islamic terrorism both overseas and on Australian soil not only represent a physical threat; the nihilistic and evil ideology underpinning terrorist acts like 9/11, the murder of Christians by Islamic state and the Sydney siege threaten democratic values and beliefs.

Apologists for those seeking to destroy our way of life refuse to acknowledge the true nature of Islamic terrorism, preferring to blame Western culture, supposedly, for excluding and marginalising disaffected groups whose only recourse is to turn to violence.

The cultural-left, instead of talking about the strengths and benefits of Western culture, engage in a narrative of self-recrimination and self-doubt.

Whereas our universities and our schools were once committed to the pursuit of what Matthew Arnold describes as "the best which has been thought and said", the impact of deconstruction and postmodernism means there are no longer any truths that we can hold in common or consider absolute.

The established disciplines of knowledge, instead of having any inherent meaning or worth, are simply "socio-cultural constructs that enforce false consciousness and the hegemony of the ruling class".

The impact of these changes on our universities and schools is significant and profound. Whereas previous generations celebrated our unique way of life, the cultural-left argues that Western civilisation is simply one culture among many.

Cultural relativism dictates that the way of life associated with our Western heritage and traditions is no longer superior or preferable. If true, one wonders on what basis we can say no to child brides, female circumcision and theocratic government as in Iran and Saudi Arabia.

Complicating matters further for is the inability or unwillingness of many conservatives to engage in what John Howard described as the battle of ideas.

As noted by Edwin Dyga in *Quadrant* magazine, such is the influence of the cultural-left dominated media, educational institutions, entertainment industry and progressive political parties that it takes a brave person to swim against the tide and to question prevailing orthodoxies.

While always couched in terms of equity and social justice, in an attempt to create a utopia on this earth, the reality is that the cultural-left's agenda is driven by the politics of pragmatism, envy and a thirst for power.

In its more extreme form, and so graphically portrayed in George Orwell's *Animal Farm*, the socialist ideal of "from each according to his ability, to each according to his need" eventually deteriorates into a cruel, violent and unjust system no different from that which has been overthrown.

No amount of propaganda, misplaced ideology or double think can disguise the harsh and brutal reality of Stalin's gulag, Mao's famines that killed millions and Pol Pot's killing fields.

By contrast, the cultural capital associated with Western civilisation, as Arnold said, embodies "the best which has been thought and said in the world".

Culture, while also referring to a way of life, in its deepest and most profound sense deals with wisdom, truth, reason and moral and spiritual values and beliefs. Over some thousands of years Western culture has become codified into a range of academic disciplines and artistic and creative activities, both theoretical and practical.

Each discipline and each activity address fundamental truths about the nature of reality, the purpose of life, what it means to be fulfilled, how to decide right from wrong and what constitutes the good life.

Western culture and its grand narrative also embody an approach to reason and rationality based on a scientific and empirical method of testing truth claims.

In opposition to witchcraft, superstition or opinion, the scientific method rests on being logical and basing conclusions on the evidence provided — evidence that can be tested and if found incorrect either revised or abandoned.

The type of scientific thinking associated with Western culture has led to dramatic and far reaching innovations and improvements in science, engineering, technology, medicine, travel and communication and food production.

Christianity and the Bible are also central to Western culture. Christ's story and the lessons from the Bible, especially the New Testament, have had, and continue to have, a profound impact on our legal and political systems, ethics and philosophy, the arts, literature and our way of life.

One only needs to see the thousands and thousands fleeing violence and death in the Middle East to the safe haven of Western Europe to realise how precious and successful Western culture is.

The Somalian activist, Ayaan Hirsi Ali, on being asked what can be done to counter Islamic terrorism, argues that the West has to "inculcate into the minds and hearts of young people an ideology or ideas of life, love, peace and tolerance".

In fact, these are the very attributes that define Western civilisation, which is why it must be defended.

How the PC left is rewriting history

There's no stopping the cultural-left's Political Correctness movement. The United Nations Committee on the Elimination of Racial Discrimination wants to ban one of Netherland's long cherished children's characters Black Pete.

Black Pete, a figure with a black-face and gold earring, accompanies St Nicholas at Christmas time handing out treats to grateful children. Apparently, the danger is that people of colour will be offended because of the negative stereotype portrayed associated with slavery.

Children's books, songs and fairy tales are also victims of the PC movement. A Victorian primary school changed the lyrics to *Kookaburra sits on the old gum tree* because the line "Gay your life must be" was in danger of upsetting the LGBTQI thought-police.

Little Black Sambo has long disappeared from library shelves, Enid Blyton's *The Three Gollywogs* is listed as one of the ten most politically incorrect children's books and *Tintin in the Congo* is attacked for promoting racist views linked to European imperialism.

Kenneth Branagh's 2015 film *Cinderella* is also decidedly politically incorrect as feminists argue it promotes an unrealistic body image to young girls and, like Shakespeare's *Romeo and Juliet*, privileges heterosexual relationships.

Arising out of the counter-culture movement of the '70s and '80s that dominated university campuses across Europe, England, America and Australia the PC movement argues that traditional institutions like the family, the church, universities and schools are misogynist, patriarchal, elitist, Eurocentric and Christian.

PC has long been the dominant narrative that stifles any disagreement or debate. One of Australia's greatest historians, Geoffrey Blainey, during the mid to late '80s was run out of Melbourne University's History Department for questioning the rate of Asian immigration.

Fred Hollows, who committed his life to curing blindness in Aboriginal communities, was attacked during the early '90s for daring to suggest the HIV and AIDS were closely associated with homosexuality.

In his 1996 ABC Boyer Lectures the Canberra-based world-famous China expert, Pierre Ryckmans, was so concerned about the impact of the PC movement on academic objectivity and standards that he argued it represented the "the fully consummated demise of the university".

The University of Western Australia cancelled the research centre involving Bjorn Lomborg, supposedly, because he was a climate change sceptic. Ignored is that Lomborg admits global warming is a significant issue that needs to be addressed.

And on American college campuses Political Correctness is alive and well as proven by the emergence of 'trigger warnings'; a situation where so-called victim groups and individuals have to be safeguarded from encountering literature that might engender a sense of disadvantage or emotional and psychological stress.

Trigger warnings, much like warnings on cigarette packets about cancer and death, signal that what is about to be read, viewed or listened to is potentially offensive.

Mark Twain's classic *Huckleberry Finn*, for example, offends Americans of colour because Jim, the runaway slave, is described as a 'nigger'. Ignored is that Twain clearly supports Jim in seeking his freedom as proven by Huck's change of heart about slavery.

One only imagines what the feminists would make of Marvell's poem *To His Coy Mistress* where the poet argues the lovers should seize the moment and consummate their relationship: "Now let us sport us while we may, And now, like amorous birds of prey, Rather at once our time devour Than languish in his slow-chapped power".

PC advocates are vocal about freedom of expression and the need to embrace diversity and difference. The hypocrisy is that at the same time anyone who questions progressive causes, like reconciliation, multiculturalism, feminism, sustainability or the LGBTQI rainbow alliance, is vilified and silenced.

Just witness the attacks on those critical of Burwood Girls High School's decision to screen the pro-gay movie *Gayby Baby* film during the normal school day. The Christian minister, Mark Powell as noted by Miranda Devine, has been especially targeted for personal abuse.

As argued by George Orwell in *Politics in the English Language* and illustrated in his novel *1984* the way language is employed is vital to the battle of ideas and to safeguard democratic liberties like freedom of expression and freedom of thought.

The greatest danger with the PC movement, like totalitarian regimes of the 'left' and the 'right', is that it seeks to censure debate, silence contrary views and ensure all conform to a group mentality where there is no opposition.

Academic centres turn on Western civilisation

David Cameron, after being first elected as the English Prime Minister in 2010, argued that the UK needed a stronger sense of identity in order to confront the menace of Islamist extremism. Atrocities in Tunisia, Kuwait and France, once again, prove how prescient he was.

The UK Prime Minister argues that to confront terrorism Western, democratic nations, in addition to increased security and eliminating physical threats, need to champion a "more active, more muscular liberalism".

Muscular liberalism involves acknowledging and defending institutions and beliefs such as the Westminster parliamentary system, natural law and Christian values such as the sanctity of life and the separation of church and state.

Such institutions and beliefs are grounded in Western civilisation, a way of life that ensures peace, prosperity and basic legal and political rights such as 'life, liberty and the pursuit of happiness'. Unfortunately, many cultural relativists in the West appear either incapable or unwilling to defend such values and beliefs.

Today Western civilisation, especially Judeo-Christianity, is criticised by many from the cultural-left. Take the example of the Australian Curriculum Studies Association (ACSA) — the peak body representing many of Australia's academics, subject associations and educational researchers with a special interest in the school curriculum.

In response to recommendation 15 in the Final Report of the review of the Australian national curriculum calling for a greater emphasis on Western civilisation ACSA argues it is wrong to privilege one civilisation over another.

ACSA justifies its response by arguing, "Many Australians do not have a Western, so termed 'Judeo-Christian heritage'. Such a recommendation ignores the multicultural, multi-faith composition of contemporary Australia, and recommends privileging one over another, when any pluralist would recognise that one interpretation of civilisation and its heritage should stand equally and alongside any other".

In the ACSA's journal, *Curriculum Perspectives*, Vol 35, No 1, Deborah Henderson from the Queensland University of Technology criticises recommendation 15 for its "Eurocentrism" and, supposedly, for marginalising "those forms of knowledge from or about other cultural traditions".

In the same journal Michael Kindler, a one-time head of the ACT's curriculum branch, argues that because Australia is a multi-cultural, multi-faith society Judeo-Christianity is simply one belief system alongside "Islamic, Buddhism, agnostic and atheist beliefs".

Ignored, based on the 2011 Census, is that Christianity is the major Australian religion at 61% compared to Buddhism at 2.5%, Islam at 2.2%, Hinduism 1.3%, Judaism 0.5% and no religion 22.3%.

ACSA is not alone in its criticism of recommendation 15. Tony Taylor from the University of Technology in Sydney argues that Judeo-Christianity is a neoconservative "fabricated myth" and "a Cold War rhetorical fiction". One wonders what Taylor makes of His Holiness Pope Francis' use of the term "Judaeo-Christian tradition" multiple times in his Encyclical Letter On Care For Our Common Home?

David Zyngier from Monash University is also concerned about any changes to the national curriculum when he argues, "This new emphasis however on the Bible and the so-called Judeo-Christian heritage is very worrying. The concept Judeo-Christian is something that is insulting to both religions".

The first point to make, as noted by Pierre Ryckmans in his 1996 ABC Boyer Lectures, is that "multiculturalism is a pleonasm and a tautology". Ryckmans argues, with one or two exceptions, that all cultures are multicultural as, in order to prosper and grow, they incorporate a range of external influences, beliefs, innovations and customs.

Western civilisation is a variegated culture, since the time of ancient Greece and Rome, that has drawn on and assimilated a host of different beliefs, ideas and cultural influences. In relation to English language and literature, for example, influences include Germanic, Scandinavian, Norman French, French, Latin and Celtic.

At the same time, to accept that inherently Western cultures like Australia are multicultural should not lead to cultural relativism, a belief that it is impossible to discriminate or to make judgements of relative worth.

The Indian caste system and practices such as sati, child brides and infanticide are morally and ethically unacceptable and run counter to concepts such as natural law and the sanctity of life that are products of Western civilisation.

The more extreme forms of Islamic fundamentalism such as female genital mutilation, killing unbelievers, banning homosexuality and carrying out a fatwa against those condemned for offending the Prophet are also barbaric and have no place in Western civilisation.

Concepts like the separation of church and state, habeas corpus, freedom of speech, religion and political beliefs and the separation of powers between the legislature, the judiciary and the executive are historically grounded in Western political and legal theory and practice.

As proven by events such as the Spanish Inquisition, the European slave trade, colonial imperialism and the Holocaust it is true that Western civilisation is far from perfect but, at the same time it is unique in that it has the ability to critique and overcome cruelty and injustice.

As noted by Arthur M. Schlesinger, Jr, "The crimes committed by the West have produced their own antidotes. They have produced great movements to end slavery, to raise the status of women, to abolish torture, to combat racism, to defend freedom of inquiry and expression, to advance personal liberty and human rights".

Mary Wollstonecraft's A Vindication of the Rights of Women, Tom Paine's Declaration of the Rights of Man and the American Declaration of Independence could only have been written by those immersed in Western civilisation and thought.

The concept of natural law illustrated by Magna Carta, for example, can be traced back to the British jurist Henry de Bracton, the Archbishop of Canterbury Stephen Langton, the Italian priest Saint Thomas Aquinas and to the view of law that evolved during the time of the Roman Empire.

As Cicero argued so many years ago, "True law is Reason, right and natural, commanding people to fulfil their obligations and prohibiting and deterring them from doing wrong. Its validity is universal; it is immutable and eternal. Its commands and prohibitions apply effectively to good men, and those uninfluenced by them are bad".

A belief in what the Declaration of Independence describes as "certain unalienable Rights" including "Life, Liberty and the pursuit of Happiness" is based on natural law — drawing on both secular and religious arguments — and helps distinguish Western civilisation from totalitarian and barbarian ideologies such as Islamic state.

Instead of myth, superstition or heresy associated with primitive cultures and civilisations Western thought is also based on reason. Best illustrated by scientific rationalism where the process is one of testing truth claims against what can or cannot be empirically proven.

Copernicus and Galileo proved that the earth was not the centre of the universe and European and British sailors were able to circumnavigate the world using inventions like the sextant and chronometer.

Western physics, mathematics and technology have been employed to split the atom, put a man on the moon and are responsible for planes staying in the sky and bridges not collapsing. Ironically, Western civilisation also champions universities as centres of learning that since the Medieval period have acted as sanctuaries for academic freedom, debate and research.

These are the very universities in which so many academics espousing cultural relativism, like cuckoos in a nest, champion anti-Western postmodern and post-colonial theories

Singing the national anthem should be compulsory

How far should we go in accepting diversity and difference, the new code for multiculturalism, and allow immigrants to pursue their own values and customs? And to what extent should all those who live here be integrated into Australian society and accept the nation's way of life?

Clearly there are some like the principal of Cranbourne Carlisle Primary School in Broadmeadows who believe multiculturalism means accepting other cultural practices and not enforcing ceremonies celebrating Australian national identity.

This week, the principal, Cheryl Irving, told Shiite Muslim students that they could excuse themselves from singing *Advance Australia Fair* if they were observing Muharram, a month of mourning that marks the death of Imam Hussein, because during this time, Shiites do not participate in joyful events, including listening to music or singing.

The principal is wrong. All those who live in Australia, especially immigrants, should accept that Australian society is unique and that the types of freedoms and basic rights we often take for granted must be celebrated and upheld.

Schools holding a weekly assembly, where the flag is raised and students sing *Advance Australia Fair*, is an essential part of Australian identity and should be compulsory. All students should also be taught that Australia is a Western, liberal democracy that, while being secular in nature, owes much to its Judaeo-Christian heritage and traditions.

The reality is that the type of tolerance associated with having a diverse society embracing various religions, values and cultural practices depends on accepting a common set of institutions, ideas and beliefs that allow such tolerance to exist in the first place.

Our political and legal systems, that we have inherited largely from Britain, are based on concepts such as sanctity of life, freedom of expression and the right to go about one's business free of coercion or fear of violence.

And such a society has not happened by accident. Australia owes a good deal to Western civilisation and a history that extends back to seminal events like the Renaissance, the Reformation and the Enlightenment and to ancient Rome and Greece.

Concepts such as natural law and the belief that all have the right to life, liberty and the pursuit of happiness are also in many ways culturally specific and not universally upheld.

As noted by The Human Freedom Index, countries where citizens have the greatest economic and political freedom are in Europe and the Anglosphere, and citizens who are most oppressed live in counties such as Pakistan, Saudi Arabia and Iran.

One only needs to observe the death and destruction in Syria and Iraq and how Islamic terrorist organisations like Islamic State and Boko Haram brutally murder Christians and abduct and rape young girls to realise how fortunate we are.

To accept otherwise and to argue that all cultures are of equal value and worth leads to cultural relativism and the fragmentation of society. It should not surprise anyone that British Prime Minister David Cameron and German Chancellor Angela Merkel both argue that multiculturalism has failed.

In a speech Cameron, after noting the 2000 cases of female genital mutilation that occurred in one year and that some British Muslim schools are guilty of indoctrinating students, argues that Britain is a Christian country and all who live there must accept British values.

"We are all British", Cameron says, "we respect democracy and the rule of law. We believe in freedom of speech, freedom of the press, freedom of worship, equal rights regardless of race, sex, sexuality or faith."

Submissions to the 2014 review of the Australian national curriculum argued in a similar vein: that in subjects like history and civics, students should be taught that Australia is a secular society with a strong Judaeo-Christian heritage, unlike theocratic societies like Iran and Saudi Arabia.

The reality is that it is the Bible that is the seminal text of Western nations like Australia and it continues to have a significant impact on our moral and spiritual values, in addition to much of our music, art and literature.

Samuel Johnson is attributed with the saying, "Patriotism is the last refuge of the scoundrel" and some might argue that singing the national anthem is jingoistic and offensive to some religious beliefs and practices.

Ignored is that if Australia is to be a cohesive, open and prosperous society instead of one where disunity prevails, future citizens must be taught to acknowledge and celebrate our national institutions and what makes us unique.

How to teach what it means to be Australian

Now that Islamic State terrorism has arrived on our soil it's time to ask the question: what does it mean to be Australian?

There's no denying that during the 1950s and 1960s the prevailing mood was nationalistic and pro-British. When I was at school, for example, every Monday morning at assembly we neatly lined up in rows, saluted the flag and sang *God save the Queen.*

Celebrating diversity is only feasible when there is a willingness to commit to the values and beliefs that underpin and sustain tolerance.

With our hands on our hearts children would then recite the oath of allegiance and promise to "cheerfully obey my parents, teachers and the law". The world map on the back of our workbooks was covered in red, proving that the sun never set on the British Commonwealth.

Fast-forward to Al Grasby and the Whitlam government in the early 1970s when multiculturalism was born and everything began to change. Against the background of Vietnam moratoriums and the counter-culture movement, what Geoffrey Blainey described as the "three cheers view" of history became superfluous and representative of a bygone era.

Australia had to cut the umbilical cord to Westminster and assert its independence. As a result of waves of post-war immigration we were now a nation of diverse cultures where those who came to live here were free to celebrate and hold on to what makes them unique.

Governments spent millions resourcing classroom materials and programs to celebrate diversity and difference. Saluting the flag was jingoistic, the bronzed ANZAC a caricature (or, at worst misogynistic) and British settlement an invasion.

At its extreme, multiculturalism championed the view that all cultures are equal and that embracing tolerance and respect meant that it was impossible to discriminate and argue that some beliefs or practices are un-Australian.

Initiatives like the Howard Government's Discovering Democracy and Values Education programmes, where children were taught to appreciate the institutions, values and beliefs that make us unique and bind us as a nation, were derided as conservative, Anglophobic and binary.

The result? Generations of young people are ignorant of the nation's history and fail to see why democracy, for all its limitations, should be preferred before all other forms of government.

Worse still, even though limited to a radicalised few, is the fact that there are those born and who have grown up here who place their allegiance to foreign, terrorist ideologies before a commitment to being Australian.

What's to be done? The first thing is to jettison the postmodern, deconstructed belief that it is impossible to discriminate and to argue that some cultural practices are unacceptable.

Cultural relativism is inherently contradictory — if it is impossible to argue that any one particular view of culture is preferable or superior, then on what basis can advocates of cultural relativism argue that their version should prevail?

Cultural relativism, like the argument put by the Green's Senator Peter Whish-Wilson that it is wrong to use the word "terrorism" as it demonises people, also fails the pub or barbecue test.

Forcing child brides to marry, female circumcision, refusing to accept the division between church and state and believing that anyone not of your religion or faith doesn't deserve to live are cultural practices that Australians reject.

Secondly, as argued by Chris Bowen when Minister for Immigration and Citizenship in a 2011 speech to the Sydney Institute, those who come to live here, while free to retain a sense of their own identity and culture, must abide by Australian laws and values.

Bowen argues: "Those who arrive in Australia are invited to continue to celebrate their cultures and traditions ... However, if there is any inconsistency between these cultural values and the values of individual freedom and the rule of law, then these traditional Australian values win out."

Celebrating diversity and difference is only feasible when there is a willingness to commit to and protect the values and beliefs that underpin and sustain tolerance and accepting others.

And such beliefs, values and institutions have not developed by accident or in a vacuum.

They are associated with a unique form of government that has evolved from Westminster Parliament, a legal system based on common law and a moral code of behaviour drawing on Judeo-Christian beliefs and significant historical events like the Reformation and the Enlightenment.

What creeds should we hold in common? Is being Australian a feature of your geographical location, your genealogy or your culture?

Joseph Furphy, in a letter to the *Bulletin* magazine's editor JF Archibald, describes *Such is Life* as follows: "temper, democratic; bias, offensively Australian". In answering the question: What creeds should we hold in common? Furphy's description encapsulates what is unique about our culture and what we should celebrate as a nation.

Australia has a long and proud history of democratic freedom, based on the Westminster parliamentary system and English common law. Since federation we have led the world in introducing reforms such as universal franchise, the old age pension and a conciliation and arbitration system based on 'a fair go for all'.

One only needs to travel abroad or to look at our music, literature, film and other cultural expressions like fashion and sport, to appreciate what is unique and distinctive about the Australian character. Laconic, open and practical, egalitarian, but also competitive and, compared to closed societies, tolerant to a degree that is sometimes counterproductive.

While our society and culture have evolved, especially since the end of the Second World War as a result of our immigration policy, and it is no longer fashionable to acknowledge the values we hold in common, the reality is that Australia, in a region surrounded by instability and violence, is an outpost of Western Civilisation characterised by an open and free society.

Those on the 'cultural-left' deny this heritage. Especially when it comes to education, much of the curriculum associated with studies of society and the environment (SOSE) states that Australian culture and society is characterised by diversity and difference.

As noted by Kenan Malik in *All cultures are not equal*, the prevailing intellectual climate in the West is to disparage what we should hold most dear, he states:

> To be radical today is to display disenchantment with all that is 'Western' — by which means modernism and the ideas of the Enlightenment — in the name of

'diversity' and 'difference'. The modernist project of pursuing a rational, scientific understanding of the natural and social world is now widely regarded as a dangerous fantasy, even as oppressive.

Instead of celebrating Australia's Western tradition, including our Anglo-Celtic heritage, students are told that we have always been multicultural and that all cultures are of equal worth. On reading the SOSE documents the focus is on what divides us, instead of what we share in common.

The Tasmanian curriculum, when explaining what is meant by social responsibility, emphasises the need to endorse "multiple perspectives" and "diverse views".

The South Australian curriculum, in outlining the importance of students understanding cultural and global connections, also emphasises "diversity" and "difference", as does the ACT curriculum, under the heading Australian perspectives, when it says that students should experience the "diversity of Australian life".

The way studying Australian history is described in the Victorian curriculum also stresses diversity, multiple influences and the multicultural nature of Australian society — with the exception of Aboriginal and Torres Strait Islander communities that are given special treatment.

The Italian philosopher, Marcello Pera describes the argument in favour of cultural relativism as follows:

> The notion that the judgement of cultures or civilizations constitutes an invalid mode of inquiry has been put forward, most notoriously, by the school of thought known as relativism. Various names have been given to this school today: post-enlightenment thinking, post-modernism, "weak thought",

deconstructionism. The labels have changed, but the target is always the same: to proclaim that there are no grounds for our values and no solid proof or argument establishing that any one thing is better or more valid that another.

While it is true that Aborigines settled in this continent years before Europeans and migrants from many different races and cultures have made this country their home, the reality is that Australia's development as a nation and its legal, political institutions and language are Anglo-Celtic in origin and deeply influenced by our Judeo-Christian heritage.

Notwithstanding the cultural-left's dislike of assimilation, research shows that the sons and daughters of migrants prefer to intermarry and to identify themselves with the broader Australian community instead of forming separatist enclaves.

Post Bali bombings and post 9/11 the weaknesses and flaws in cultural relativism are many. Firstly, arguing there is nothing inherently worthwhile about particular cultures ignores the fact that some cultural practices — female circumcision, misogynism and Sati (where wives throw themselves on their husband's funeral pyres) — are wrong and un-Australian.

Also ignored is that the very values of tolerance, compassion, openness and civility that ensure Australia's continued peace and stability are culturally specific and based on our Western heritage. Much of Mankind's history is a story of bitter and violent warfare, civil unrest and destruction, Australia, by comparison, has a settled and peaceful record.

In a world of increasing globalisation, where international travel, music, film, the internet and other forms of entertainment make national borders redundant and impose a homogenous view of culture, the danger is that young Australians remain ignorant of who and what we are as a nation.

If nothing else, the return of the History wars, sparked by the 2006 Canberra History Summit, provides an opportunity to ask the question: what should young people be taught about the past and what is the narrative that best tells our story?

Many argue that the type of grand narrative associated with a celebratory, Anglo-Celtic, Christian view of Australian society should be condemned as 'conservative, Eurocentric and nationalistic' and of little value. I disagree.

In the same way Winston Churchill argued that while democracy might be flawed, it is superior to any alternatives, in relation to Western Civilisation, I would argue that while it is far from perfect, it is certainly superior to the rest.

THE DANGERS OF ISLAMIC FUNDAMENTALISM

For the fundamental problem is that the majority of otherwise peaceful and law-abiding Muslims are unwilling to acknowledge, much less to repudiate, the theological warrant for intolerance and violence embedded in their religious texts.[2]

2   Ayaan Hirsi Ali. 2015. *Heretic Why Islam Needs A Reformation Now.* Harper Collins Publishers. Sydney. P 13.

Our country, our rules: Citizenship program changes welcome

It might be two years too late but finally the Australian government appears to be learning from the European and UK experiences of the damaging and destabilising effects of multiculturalism, unrestricted immigration, and Islamic terrorism.

Two years ago, the German Chancellor Angela Merkel argued multiculturalism was a failed policy that led "to parallel societies" and that immigrants must learn German and live by German values.

At the same time Prime Minister David Cameron argued that Britain was a Christian nation and that all who lived there must accept that its political and legal institutions and way of life are paramount and must be defended.

After last month arguing that "Australia is the most successful multicultural society in the world" and we are not defined by "race, religion, or culture" Prime Minister Malcolm Turnbull appears to be learning from what is happening overseas.

The PM now argues that Australia's migration program must better contribute to "our social cohesion while enhancing our security" and as a condition of citizenship migrants must embrace "Australian values" and "our cultural values".

If the Prime Minister is serious then the Australian Citizenship Pledge is a good place to start. Prospective citizens pledge their "loyalty to Australia and its people, whose democratic beliefs I share, whose rights and liberties I respect, and whose laws I will uphold and obey".

Compare that to the American Oath of Allegiance where future citizens have to "renounce and abjure allegiance and fidelity to any foreign prince, potentate, state or sovereignty" and defend the United States "against all enemies, foreign, and domestic" and it's clear which is the stronger.

The British Oath of Allegiance is also more direct and couched in stronger language compared to the Australian Pledge. It states "I will give my loyalty to the United Kingdom and respect its rights and freedoms. I will uphold its democratic values. I will observe its laws faithfully and fulfil my duties and obligations as a British citizen".

In both the US and the British pledges, it's clear that immigrants wanting citizenship must fully embrace and defend the beliefs, values, and institutions of their newly adopted country. Holding on to enmities and hostilities from overseas or importing unacceptable customs and traditions are not allowed.

It is also vital that those who live in Australia acknowledge and celebrate what Prime Minister Turnbull refers to as "our cultural values". Not all cultures are the same or worthy of the same respect.

Australia, compared to our Asian neighbours and Islamic countries in the Middle East, is a Western liberal democracy that owes its origins to our Judaeo-Christian heritage and a history intimately associated with the rise of Western civilisation and the Anglo-sphere.

Whether the separation between church and state, the inherent dignity of each person or the right to "life, liberty, and the pursuit of happiness" the reality is that our culture is unique in its ability to protect our way of life.

As a result of inheriting British common law and a Westminster parliamentary system based on separation of powers and the people's right to choose their elected representatives, it should not surprise that Australia scores 98 out of 100 on the Freedom House's scale measuring which nations enjoy the most freedom.

Prime Minister Turnbull argues that Australia "needs to attract people who will embrace our values and positively contribute regardless of (their) nationality or religious beliefs". Mirroring events in the UK, Europe, and the US it's obvious that the government's commitment to multiculturalism is being redefined.

Placating evil is not tolerance

Tim Soutphommasane, when Australia's Race Discrimination Commissioner, argued in the Fairfax Press: "Every member of our society should be free to live without fear of discrimination. This includes being free to practise their religion, as guaranteed by section 116 of the Constitution".

Wrong.

While the Constitution states "The Commonwealth shall not make any law for establishing any religion, or for imposing any religious observance, or for prohibiting the free exercise of any religion" those responsible would not accept that all religious beliefs should be tolerated.

The reality is that not all religions are peaceful and tolerant and it's clear that some practices and beliefs are un-Australian.

The Hindu caste system discriminates against 'untouchables' and the system of dowry, where husbands demand money and gifts from their prospective wives' families, still leads to violence and death.

Best illustrated by Ayaan Hirsi Ali's latest book, *Heratic*, it's also true that Islamic fundamentalism is inherently violent.

While arguing that the majority of Muslims are "peaceful and law-abiding" Hirsi Ali cites multiple examples of unacceptable religious practices.

Based on her own experience as a child growing up in Somalia Hirsi Ali describes the widespread practice of female genital mutilation and arranged marriages.

And her experience is not unique, according to the World Health Organisation "More than 200 million girls and women alive today have been cut in 30 countries in Africa, the Middle East and Asia".

In England, Prime Minister David Cameron admits "20,000 children are still at risk" and one Australian organisation suggests up to "three girls a day are born in Australia who are at high risk".

Hirsi Ali also writes that in Pakistan, those who blaspheme against the Prophet are "punishable by death", in Saudi Arabia "churches and synagogues are outlawed", in Iran "stoning is an acceptable punishment" and in Brunei, under Sharia law, "homosexuality is punishable by death".

It's clear that not all religions support and protect the rights and freedoms we take for granted.

Instead of cultural relativism, so much favoured by the cultural-left, we should acknowledge that some religious practices are beyond the pale and that Western culture and Christianity are preferable.

Australia is a Western, liberal democracy, based on the Westminster parliamentary system and Christianity underpins our political and legal systems. The Constitution's Preamble refers to "Almighty God" and parliaments around Australia begin with the Lord's Prayer.

Concepts like sanctity of life, commitment to the common good, the separation of Church and state and free will owe as

much to the New Testament as to the Enlightenment and
political philosophers like John Stuart Mill.

And while there is no doubt that Western culture and
Christianity are far from perfect, as argued by Arthur M
Schlesinger, "The crimes committed by the West have
produced their own antidotes. They have produced great
movements to end slavery, to raise the status of women, to
abolish torture, to combat racism, and to advance personal
liberty and human rights".

Foolish to deny what makes us powerful

The alleged Christmas Day plot by Islamic terrorists targeting
Flinders Street Station, St Paul's Cathedral and Federation
Square should not come as a surprise.

Other Australian examples include the 2002 Bali bombings,
the Holsworthy Barracks terror plot, the Lindt Café siege in
Sydney and the murder of Curtis Cheng outside the Parramatta
Police Station.

Proven by the 9/11 attacks in America, the London bombings in 2005, the 2015 Paris attacks and the 2016 attack in Nice
where a truck was driven into crowds of civilians, it's clear that
fundamentalist Islam is committed to destroying Western, liberal democracies and our way of life.

And while Premier Daniel Andrews appears incapable of
connecting the dots (describing the Christmas Day plot as "an
act of evil" instead of an act of Islamic terrorism) there is no
doubt that aspects of the Islamic religion are inherently violent.

As argued by David Cameron when he was Britain's prime
minister "simply denying any connection between the religion

of Islam and the extremists doesn't work ... it is an exercise in futility to deny that".

Not only did Cameron argue that fundamentalist Islam represented a religious threat, he also argued that England was a Christian nation and everyone should accept the rule of law, the Westminster parliamentary system and the British way of life.

The Somalian-born activist Ayaan Hirsi Ali makes a similar point to Cameron in her book Heretic when she argues, "Islam is not a religion of peace". While acknowledging the vast majority of Muslims want to coexist peacefully with others, Ali details aspects of the Koran that are a threat to Western civilisation.

Examples include the Koran's hostility to women and homosexuals and the concept of dhimmi — under which non-Muslims who have been conquered face the choice of converting to Islam, paying heavy taxes or death.

Other examples include Islamic groups like IS involved in genocide, murdering thousands of Christians and other non-believers and the terrorist group Boko Haram kidnapping and enslaving more than 200 Nigerian schoolgirls.

Coptic Christians are also being killed and their churches and cathedrals destroyed in Egypt simply because Christianity is not acceptable to Islamic extremists.

In the book *111 Questions on Islam*, the point is also made that unlike the Bible, where different interpretations and disagreements are allowed, the words spoken in the Koran are directly from Allah and must not be challenged.

Those who question or insult the Koran such as the novelist Salman Rushdie are punishable by death. The governor of Jakarta, Basuki "Ahok" Tjahaja Purnama, faced trial for suggesting there is nothing in the Koran forbidding Muslims voting for a governor who is Christian.

While Western nations face an external threat represented by Islamic terrorism, there are also those within our community seeking to undermine our way of life.

Like Premier Andrews, who refuses to admit the link between terrorist acts and fundamentalist Islam, there are many in our media and in our universities refusing to admit that aspects of the Koran are hostile to Western civilisation.

Islamic apologists appear on ABC radio and television and in the Fairfax Press arguing that Islam is not a threat and labelling those critical of the Koran as Islamophobic.

The book *Learning From One Another: Bringing Muslim Perspectives Into Australian Schools*, produced by the University of Melbourne, argues that Australian schools are guilty of teaching history that privileges a "Eurocentric version of history".

Australia's national curriculum, instead of celebrating the unique benefits of Western civilisation, argues in favour of diversity and difference (the new code for multiculturalism) and that all cultures are equal.

Ignored is that all cultures are not equal and that Western liberal democracies like Australia are unique. Having inherited English common law and a Westminster form of government ensures that all citizens are equal before the law and have the right to life, liberty and the pursuit of happiness.

It's no accident that, according to the American-based Freedom House, Western nations are among the freest in the world, guaranteeing liberties such as freedom of speech and religion, universal voting, the concept of innocent until proven guilty and the right to own property.

While we are a secular society, it is also true that Christian concepts like the sanctity of life, free will, seeking good instead of evil and committing to the common good are Western in nature.

By comparison countries in our region such as China, Vietnam, Cambodia, Lao PDR and Myanmar are totalitarian regimes where the freedoms we take for granted are suppressed.

Unlike Islam, that has remained unchanged for hundreds of years, it is also true that Western civilisation has experienced periods of dramatic upheaval and change — including the Renaissance, the Enlightenment, the Reformation, the Industrial Revolution and the advent of the digital age.

Western nations are among the most prosperous and economically advanced, where science and technology have combined to put a man on the moon, split the atom, cure diseases and increase life expectancy to record levels. Let's acknowledge, defend and celebrate what we have achieved.

Islam must address its women problem

There's no doubt that Tony Abbott's speech in memory of the British Prime Minister Margaret Thatcher caused consternation, anger and disbelief among Australia's left-leaning commentariat.

In part, Abbott argues "no country or continent can open its borders to all comers without fundamentally weakening itself. This is the risk that the countries of Europe now run through misguided altruism".

The former Prime Minister also makes the point that what makes Western countries so peaceful and prosperous are values and institutions that "are not the accidents of history but the product of values painstakingly discerned and refined, and of practices carefully cultivated and reinforced over hundreds of years".

Sabine Wolff on the Jesuit's website, Eureka, condemns the speech as "a truly stunning example or revisionism, hubris and utterly confused ideology". Waleed Aly in the Fairfax media describes Abbott's speech as morally bereft and Adam Gartrell, also from Fairfax, describes the speech as "negative and extreme" and "simplistic and misleading".

Wrong. Given events including Islamic States attacks in Paris, where 130 were murdered, and the New Year's violence in Cologne where Syrian and North African immigrants assaulted over five hundred women including 237 sexual offences, it's clear that Abbott's speech was both prescient and anything but misleading.

And Abbott is not alone in warning about the dangers of illegal immigration and the need to defend the values and institutions that make Western civilisation so unique and the destination of choice for so many refugees — both legal and illegal.

In England Prime Minister Cameron argues that anyone wanting to live in England must accept and live by British values such as the rule of law, freedom of the individual and respect for others and the need for social cohesion and stability.

Cameron also argues that Britain, while accepting other religions and faiths, is essentially a Christian nation and that the school curriculum should teach that Christianity is the major religion.

The German President Joachin Gauck warns that Germany's refugee crisis represents a greater challenge than uniting East and West Germany after the fall of the Berlin Wall and that refugees should integrate into German society.

As well as arguing values like equal rights for women and homosexuals and placing secular law above religious affiliations are "not negotiable" Gauck warns that "tolerance for intolerance is not acceptable".

Angela Merkel, the German Chancellor, while being attacked for accepting over one million refuges, argues in a similar vein when she says "Those who seek refuge with us also have to respect our laws and traditions, and learn to speak German" and that "Multiculturalism leads to parallel societies, and therefore multiculturalism remains a grand delusion."

What can Australia learn from events in Europe? The first thing to understand is that nation states have every right to protect their borders and that a government's priority must be to protect its citizens and to promote social cohesion and stability.

It is also vital to understand that Australia's policy of multi-culturalism, historically speaking, is relatively new. Promoting diversity and difference became the dominant policy during the early 70's when Gough Whitlam proclaimed that "Australia is in reality a multicultural nation".

For most of the period since Federation in 1901 migrants where expected to assimilate and to accept Australian values and institutions like the rule of law, parliamentary democracy, freedom and respect for the individual and the separation between church and state.

While pushed under the guise of tolerating and respecting difference it's also important to realise that the underside of multiculturalism is political branch stacking and a billion-dollar industry involving rent seekers and self-serving ethnic organisations and community groups.

As proven by the New Year attacks in Germany where so many women feared for their lives and their safety it is also vital to accept that not all cultures are equal and that there are some cultural practices and beliefs that are un-Australian.

The reality is that there are some elements of the Islamic religion that treat women as second rate. Extracts from

The Qur'an published by Oxford University Press include statements like:

"If any of your women commit a lewd act, call four witnesses from among you, then, if they testify to their guilt, keep the women at home until death comes to them or until God shows them another way."

"If you fear high-handedness from your wives, remind them (of the teaching of God), then ignore them when you go to bed, then hit them."

"Concerning your children, God commands you that a son should have the equivalent share of two daughters."

If taken literally such commands represent a significant setback to the hard-fought rights and freedoms women in the West have won and that grant them such a high degree of freedom and equality.

Time for schools to stop the spread of extremism

In 2014 in Britain it was described as the Trojan Horse affair, a situation involving a number of Muslim schools in Birmingham where students were being indoctrinated with Islamic fundamentalism and extremism.

Such were the concerns about students being radicalised that Prime Minister David Cameron ordered schools to be investigated and that the national curriculum teach an objective and balanced view of religion, especially Christianity.

The subsequent inquiry into the schools concluded: "There has been co-ordinated, deliberate and sustained action carried out by a number of associated individuals to introduce an intolerant and aggressive Islamic ethos into a few schools in Birmingham."

As proven by events surrounding Arthur Phillip High School, the school attended by the 15-year-old terrorist Farhad Jabar, and the 2014 video of children in Sydney with an Islamic flag shouting anti-American slogans, it's clear that some of our government schools have a similar problem.

What's to be done? One approach, as recommended by a review of the national curriculum that I co-chaired, is to give a greater focus on teaching moral and spiritual values, especially Judeo-Christianity and the benefits of Western civilisation.

Australia is a Western, liberal democratic country where, notwithstanding being a secular society, its political and legal institutions, plus way of life, can only be fully understood and appreciated in terms of our Judaeo-Christian heritage and ongoing traditions.

As argued by the late Australian China scholar Pierre Ryckmans in his 1996 ABC Boyer Lectures, you cannot appreciate and understand other religions and cultures unless you are familiar with your own.

Proven by the response of many of Australia's cultural-left education academics to the review's recommendation and published on the left-leaning The Conversation website it's clear, though, that placing a greater focus on religion in the curriculum will not be an easy matter.

Tony Taylor, from the University of Technology Sydney and on The Conversation, argues that Australia's "Judaeo-Christian heritage is a prefabricated myth" and that "the expression 'Judaeo-Christian' is actually a 1980s Cold War rhetorical fiction recently revived by the Christian Right".

Taylor argues there is nothing biased about the Australian national curriculum, even though it ignores Australia's Western heritage and Christian values by adopting a cultural relativistic position, and that nothing needs to be changed.

It also should be noted that the Australian Curriculum, Assessment and Reporting Authority — the body responsible for designing the national curriculum — endorsed a civics and citizenship curriculum that ignored the role of Christian values and community-based groups in strengthening social capital and social cohesion.

An example proving the cultural-left bias of Australia's education establishment is another piece published by The Conversation and written by Sydney University's Omid Tofighian.

Tofighian, in addition to describing the Commonwealth government's anti-radicalisation kit distributed to schools as an object of "public ridicule", argues that in order to tackle extremism in schools we must challenge the "white curriculum".

Adopting the kind of tortured logic espoused by radical postmodernist, postcolonial theory, Tofighian argues that young people attracted to terrorism are simply victims of "racism, bullying, cultural and religious blindness, misogyny and economic inequality".

Such young people, apparently, are marginalised and stigmatised by Australian society, which is guilty of reinforcing conservative and monocultural norms — and the solution, instead of addressing the real issues, is to reform the curriculum and what happens in schools.

Such a curriculum, instead of enforcing "Eurocentric notions" and "the concept of whiteness", Tofighian argues, should deconstruct the "different forms of domination and marginalisation" faced by various ethnic and racial groups that constitute society.

It also should be noted that Maurie Mulheron, president of the NSW Teachers Federation, instead of supporting the Commonwealth government's anti-radicalisation kit, attacks it as cynical exercise designed to "engender fear and intolerance".

Finally — and once again published on The Conversation — the academics Anno Halafoff and Cathy Byrne argue that religion should only be taught in government schools "as long as no one view is presented as being correct or better than another".

Taken seriously, one wonders how students will be taught how to discriminate between what is right and what is wrong in terms of moral and spiritual beliefs and values and why some religious practices, such as theocracy and subjugation of women and homosexuals, are morally indefensible.

It's clear that more needs to be done in schools to counter the pernicious and evil influence of Islamic terrorism and religious intolerance.

The challenge is to do so in a way that acknowledges Australia's Western heritage and Judaeo-Christian traditions while promoting interfaith tolerance and dialogue.

Muslims must learn Western values

The evil and barbaric killing of an innocent civilian outside the Parramatta police station, plus the fact that 100s of Australian Muslims are now fighting in the Middle East for Islamic State, proves that we are not immune from the scourge of home grown, Islamic terrorism.

What's to be done? One approach is to acknowledge that such violent and unjustified acts are isolated and in no way representative of Australia's Muslim community.

Australia is a multi-cultural, multi-faith society where different ethnic and religious groups co-exist and the acts of a demented few should not be used to vilify others of the same faith.

At the same time the question has to be asked: what can be done to counter the seductive, nihilistic urge of Islamic terrorism and to ensure that all Australians are committed to the liberal, democratic values that guarantee our peaceful and secure way of life?

One answer, as argued by British Prime Minister David Cameron, is to advocate what he terms "muscular liberalism".

When explaining the rise of Islamic terrorism Cameron argues that for far too long advocates of multiculturalism have ignored the fact that British society is unique and that celebrating diversity and difference can divide instead of unify.

Cameron argues that all those wishing to settle in the UK must adhere to British values such as "Freedom of speech. Freedom of worship. Democracy. The rule of law (and) Equal rights, regardless of race, sex or sexuality".

Such values form the common ground that underpins British society and that differentiate the UK from totalitarian, theocratic regimes like Saudi Arabia and Iran and cultural practices like female circumcision, misogyny and mistreatment of homosexuals.

In a speech at Easter, Cameron also argued that Britain is a Christian nation and that its political and legal institutions and concepts like individual liberty and a commitment to the common good derive from the Bible.

While secular humanism, illustrated by the Enlightenment, is significant Cameron argues, "the Church is not just a collection of beautiful old buildings. It is a living, active force across our country".

The English academic, Larry Siendentop in *Inventing the Individual: The Origins of Western Liberalism*, argues in a similar vein when detailing the impact of the early years of Christianity on the origins of liberal democracy and the concept of inalienable rights.

Sienentop argues that the Christian vision of the "equality of souls in the eyes of God" and concepts like free will and individual conscience are the underpinnings of modern democratic concepts such as "life, liberty and the pursuit of happiness".

In a speech titled *Extremism*, Cameron details a four-part plan to "defeat extremism and at the same time to build a stronger, more cohesive society". The British Prime Minister's plan includes teaching respect and tolerance in the school curriculum while also teaching the values and beliefs that safeguard democracy.

Secondly, Cameron argues there is no room in British society for Islamic extremists attempting to indoctrinate the young. Thirdly, while acknowledging that the overwhelming majority of Muslims are peaceful and not a threat, Cameron argues that there is a relationship between Islam and terrorism.

The Prime Minister argues it is a mistake for cultural-left academics and elements in the progressive media to portray Islam as a peaceful religion with no connection to extremism.

Cameron states "Denying any connection between the religion of Islam and the extremists doesn't work… it is an exercise in futility to deny that". Cameron continues, "We can't stand neutral in the battle of ideas. We have to back those who share our values".

Finally, Cameron argues more must be done to support moderate Muslims, including giving parents the right to confiscate passports and reaching out to the Muslim community to involve it more effectively in the political process.

The German President and the German Chancellor, Joachim Gauk and Angela Merkel respectively, are also critical of multiculturalism and argue that Muslim immigrants must assimilate into German society.

In a speech last week celebrating 25 years of unification the German Chancellor states that values such as human dignity, equal rights for women and homosexuals and respect for the secular law regardless of any religious affiliation "are not up for debate".

In the fight against Islamic extremism there is no doubt that counter-terrorism involving surveillance, intelligence gathering and monitoring suspects plays a crucial role.

Equally as important is what Cameron describes as the battle of ideas and the need to acknowledge and defend the unique nature and benefits of Western, liberal democracies like Australia and what unifies instead of what divides.

Cameron's lesson in defeating Islamism

Evidence of Islamic terrorism continues both here and overseas and Premier Baird's decision to investigate the impact of Islamic extremism on NSW schools is overdue and welcome. In 2014 the British government faced the same problem with the Trojan Horse affair.

A situation where a number of Islamic schools in Birmingham fell under the influence of Islamic terrorist propaganda and a subsequent government review confirmed there was a significant problem.

Other examples of the imminent danger represented by Islamic fundamentalism include the Victorian nurse, Adam

Brookman, who has just been extradited from NSW to face trail in Victoria for allegedly working with Islamic State militants. In 2015 police raided four homes across Melbourne suburbs investigating a plan by Islamic youth to target police on ANZAC Day. And hundreds of disaffected youth from Britain and Australia are still flocking to the Middle East to spread jihad against the West and moderate Muslims.

What's to be done? In a 2015 keynote speech titled 'Extremism' the British Prime Minister David Cameron detailed a four-point plan to "defeat extremism and at the same time build a stronger, more cohesive society".

Firstly, Cameron argues that even though Britain is a multi-faith, multicultural society like Australia everybody who lives there, especially migrants, must adopt British values and support British institutions.

Cameron argues, "We are all British. We respect democracy and the rule of law. We believe in freedom of speech, freedom of the press, freedom of worship, equal rights regardless of race, sex, sexuality or faith".

Promoting choice and diversity and the right of migrants to live their own culture only works if there is integration and a commitment to those values that underpin tolerance and equal rights. In an earlier speech Cameron also argues that Britain is a Christian country and Judeo-Christian beliefs must be supported.

Cultural practices like child brides, female genital mutilation (of which there where 5,700 reported cases in 2015-16 in Britain) and honour killings, Cameron argues, must also be seen as totally unacceptable and punished.

Secondly, the British Prime Minister argues that home grown apologists for Islamic terrorism must be dealt with.

Islamic religious leaders spreading hatred and those in schools indoctrinating students, like those in Birmingham schools in 2014, must be identified and stopped.

Thirdly, unlike those arguing that evil terrorist organisations like Islamic State have no relationship to Islam as a religion, Cameron argues there is a connection.

The Prime Minister says "simply denying any connection between the religion of Islam and the extremists doesn't work… it is an exercise in futility to deny that". Cameron goes on to say "We can't stand neutral in the battle of ideas. We have to back those who share our values".

Cameron also argues that the government needs to do more to support moderate Muslims, including giving parents the right to confiscate their children's passports. Ways must also be found to involve more Muslims in the political process.

The fourth part of Cameron's strategy to confront and overcome Islamic fundamentalism involves building a "more cohesive society, so more people feel part of it and are less vulnerable to extremism". A key part of this, Cameron suggests, involves combating what is described as "racism, discrimination or sickening Islamophobia".

To argue that all Muslims are terrorists or dangerous because of the actions of a few extremists is both false and morally wrong.

Young Muslims, in particular, need to be properly educated, find employment and given the opportunity to participate in the democratic process. Living and going to schools in suburbs segregated by ethnicity and race is also identified as a danger.

Cameron concludes his speech by arguing that all those living in Britain, regardless of culture, religion or race, must stand up for and promote "shared British values". He also argues that Muslim communities have "crucial parts to play" in promoting such values.

To date, most of Australian state and commonwealth strategies to fight Islamic terrorism has focused on military and intelligence responses. Equally as important, as argued by David Cameron, is to fight the "battle of ideas" and to promote an integrated, cohesive society with shared beliefs and values.

Many of the submissions to the 2014 review of the Australian national curriculum made the same point, hence, the recommendation to place a greater emphasis on moral and spiritual values in the curriculum, especially Judeo-Christianity and the benefits of Western civilisation.

Teaching Western values in schools helps beat Islamic extremism

Omar Hallak, the principal at Melbourne's Al-Taqwa College, is being criticised for suggesting Western countries are behind the terrorist organisation Islamic State. In Sydney a video showed children with an Islamic State flag and chanting anti-US slogans.

Given the number of Australian Muslims going overseas to fight for terrorist groups there are mounting concerns that young Muslims are being presented with a one-sided view of religion and the nature of the conflict between Islam and the West.

Evidenced by what is known as the Trojan Horse affair it is obvious that England is facing a similar problem. In 2014 a number of Muslim schools in Birmingham were accused of promoting extremist Islamic views calculated to undermine the peace and stability of British society.

The government responded by initiating an inquiry that concluded: "There has been co-ordinated, deliberate and sustained action carried out by a number of associated individuals to introduce an intolerant and aggressive Islamic ethos into a few schools in Birmingham."

As a result of the Trojan Horse affair the British Prime Minister, David Cameron, argued that all schools must teach British values.

The British Department of Education's Promoting fundamental British values as part of SMSC in schools lists these as the "values of democracy, the rule of law, individual liberty and mutual respect and tolerance of those with different faiths and beliefs".

The British document also stresses the need for "tolerance and harmony between different cultural traditions by enabling students to acquire an appreciation of and respect for their own and other cultures".

On face value, such an approach is to be recommended. As noted by the British document, embracing diversity and difference is important on the basis that it is not "acceptable for schools to promote discrimination against people or groups on the basis of their belief, opinion or background".

On a closer examination, though, and taken to its logical conclusion such an approach is flawed. To suggest that all religions, cultures and belief systems should be acknowledged and celebrated denies the fact that some beliefs and practices are unacceptable.

Female circumcision, child brides, the Indian custom of punishing a bride if her dowry is unacceptable, outlawing homosexuality, denying and punishing free speech and imposing a theocratic view of government have no place in Western, liberal, democratic societies such as Britain and Australia.

As comprehensively detailed by Ayaan Hirsi Ali the reality is that aspects of Islam, especially in places like Saudi Arabia, are misogynist and dictatorial.

To argue it is wrong to discriminate because of the belief that all cultures and belief systems are of equal value leads to cultural relativism; a situation where it is impossible to protect a unique way of life that we, in Australia, take for granted.

A second approach to the question of how to deal with diversity and difference is provided by a document titled Values, endorsed by 22 Christian leaders and presented to Britain's House of Commons.

While also endorsing values such as democracy, the rule of law, tolerance and respecting others the document argues that such values are culturally specific as they arise from "Judaeo-Christian belief, thought and practice, which has been foundational to these islands".

Qualities and ethical values such as free will, respecting the sanctity of life, caring for others, being charitable and truth telling have not arisen accidently and are not practised universally.

The document argues that British history "authenticates the role and benefits of Christian teaching and practice" illustrated by such things as the abolition of slavery and the "establishment of the rights of conscience and the consistent opposition to intimidation, coercion, corruption, tyranny and oppression".

In relation to the law, it is significant that in an interview in the March 2015 edition of *Quadrant*, the former chief justice of Australia, Murray Gleeson, states: "Many of our laws have come from religious sources, respect for human life is an obvious example."

The American Declaration of Independence provides further evidence of the significance of Christianity when it states that the unalienable rights enjoyed by all are "endowed by their Creator".

Of course, to argue that Christianity plays a central role in our society and culture is not to deny the significant influence of historical events like the Renaissance, the Reformation and the Enlightenment.

Any history of Western civilisation must also acknowledge the dark side of Christianity and the fact that secular philosophy has played a major role in the evolution and development of Western civilisation.

It is vital that Western, liberal, democratic countries like Britain and Australia as key members of the Anglosphere are clear about what makes them unique and what it is that safeguards our peace and prosperity and that we must defend.

So, the untouchables must be tolerant

Proven by the latest bizarre example, where Muslim students do not have to shake hands with females, it's clear that education's politically correct embrace of diversity and difference, the new code for multiculturalism, reigns supreme.

As reported in the *Australian* newspaper, school officials at Sydney's Hurstville Boys Campus, based on a literal interpretation of the *Hadith*, tell Muslim students that it is OK to refuse to greet females in the customary way.

So much for the Christian admonition 'When in Rome, do as the Romans do' and the fact that Australian society only prospers and grows when there is a shared understanding of what constitutes civility and good manners.

And Muslim students not shaking hands is not an isolated example. In 2015 a Victorian primary school allowed Muslim students to absent themselves during the singing of the national anthem. At the University of Melbourne Islamic groups have been given permission to segregate meetings involving males and females.

So much for the claim made on the ABC's Q&A by the Islamic activist Yassim Abdel-Magied that her religion grants women the same rights and freedoms as men and that Islam does not unfairly discriminate because of one's sexuality.

Education now embraces identity politics where the rights and privileges of particular individuals and groups nominated by the cultural-left are granted positive discrimination (except, of course, if you are a white Anglo-Celtic, Christian male happy to live in a heterosexual relationship).

Whereas in times past schools would teach all students about the values, beliefs and institutions that bind us as a nation and the debt owed to Western culture, the focus is now firmly on what divides us instead of what we share in common.

Even worse, instead of their arguments being properly analysed and evaluated, anyone questioning multicultural groupthink is quickly condemned as Islamophobic, racist and intolerant.

As noted by the UK journalist and author Patrick West "Tolerance in the name of relativism has become its own intolerance. We are commended to respect all differences and anyone who disagrees shall be shouted down, silenced or slandered as a racist. Everyone must be tolerant. And that's an order".

The Australian National Curriculum advocates identity politics and the belief that all cultures must be treated equally. Christianity, instead of being acknowledged as one of the foundation stones on which Western culture rests and continues to depend, receives the same weighting as Islam, Buddhism and Hinduism.

While the National Curriculum stipulates that subjects and areas of learning must celebrate diversity and difference, with a special focus an Asian and indigenous perspectives, scant time or attention is given to the history and significance of liberalism within the Western tradition.

The NSW 'Statement of Equity Principles' endorsed by the Education Standards Council also illustrates the way education has been captured by the cultural-left's long march through the institutions.

Whether the school syllabus, associated materials or assessment guidelines the focus is on "difference and diversity in the Australian community" where all must be respected and treated equally regardless of "cultural and linguistic heritage, gender, age, beliefs, socioeconomic status, location, sexuality or disability".

Such a relativistic stance inexorably leads to the situation where it is impossible to condemn or prohibit practices such as child brides, female circumcision and treating women as inferior to men.

In this smorgasbord of identity politics, where all cultures and beliefs systems are of equal value (except for indigenous that gets special treatment) schools are also told they must not discriminate as all students "have the right to different beliefs" and the right to experience a "positive sense of identity and self-respect".

One wonders whether the call for tolerance applies to what the past president of the Australian Federation of Islamic Councils, Haset Sali, describes as "a toxic subculture" in Muslim schools where the fear is students are being radicalised by hate preachers to carry out jihad against the apostates and non-believers.

Multiculturalism ignores the reality that some cultural practices and beliefs are un-Australian and that unless we want to follow the example of the UK and Europe, where the policy has led to ethnic ghettos, violence and social fragmentation, education must teach how to discriminate between what constitutes acceptable and unacceptable beliefs and values.

There is also the irony that they very values that cultural relativists champion, such as tolerance and respect for others, are culturally specific. The liberties and freedoms we take for granted are embedded in Western culture, our Judeo-Christian heritage and historical movements like the Enlightenment.

It is the Bible and not the Koran that says "There is neither Jew nor Greek, there is neither bond nor free, there is neither male nor female: for ye are all one in Christ Jesus".

It is also because of Western moral philosophers like Jeremy Bentham and John Stuart Mill that we have a separation between church and state and that we don't live in a theocracy like Iran, Saudi Arabia, Bahrain and Oman where sharia law prevails and basic rights are denied.

School textbooks gloss over jihad and undermine Christianity

Joseph Ratzinger, better known as Pope Benedict XVI, in Without Roots: The West, Relativism, Christianity and Islam, details the rising tide of secularism that seeks to banish Christianity from European history and the public square.

While the situation in Australia appears nowhere near as dire as Europe it is also the case here that Christianity is often misrepresented and undermined.

Especially in subjects like history and in relation to what the American political scientist, Samuel P. Huntington, terms the "clash of civilizations" the expectation is that school textbooks present a balanced, objective and impartial view of ideas, beliefs and events.

Such is not the case with textbooks like Jacaranda's *SOSE Alive 2* (2004), Oxford University Press' *Big Ideas Australian Curriculum History 8* (2012) and *Learning From One Another: Bringing Muslim Perspectives into Australian Schools* (2010).

Instead of being impartial and objective the three textbooks display a jaundiced and superficial view of Christianity.

When describing the role of the Church in Medieval times, instead of acknowledging its beneficial impact, the Jacaranda textbook presents a bleak and negative picture. The Catholic Church, supposedly, enforces its teachings by making people "terrified of going to hell", a situation where "Old people who lived alone, especially women, and people who disagreed with the Church were at great risk".

One of the role plays students are asked to role play involves imagining "that as a simple, God-fearing peasant, you have been told you were excommunicated" and, in relation to how the Church treated women, students are told "mostly they did what the Church told them to do — to be obedient wives, good mothers, and caretakers of the home".

Not only is such an interpretation of the Church's impact on women simplistic, it also judges social relations occurring in the far distant past according to contemporary ideas and beliefs.

The Jacarada book, after describing those who attacked the World Trade Center as terrorists, asks students, "Might it also be fair to say that the Crusaders who attacked the Muslim inhabitants of Jerusalem were also terrorists?".

Equating 9/11 Islamic terrorists with the early Crusaders displays a misguided and simplistic understanding of the historical circumstances surrounding the Church's desire to reclaim Jerusalem and the Holy Lands.

The Oxford textbook (2012) represents an improvement on the Jacaranda textbook as it acknowledges the beneficial impact of the Church on European civilisation. The statement is made that in medieval Europe the "church was a positive influence on societies across Europe — providing education, caring for the sick and supporting the community".

Such a positive statement is undermined by the illustration accompanying this description that depicts "heretics (people whose religious beliefs conflicted with the teachings of the Church) being burned at the stake".

The observation that "Christian beliefs and values had many positive effects on daily life, architecture, the arts and the justice system", while welcome, is also undermined by the qualification that Christian values and beliefs "also provided motivations for wars, and justifications for some people's prejudices and fears".

The portrayal of Christianity and the Catholic Church is one where wrongdoers "where doomed to hell", missionaries enforce "very strict and Catholic beliefs" and the medieval Church worked against "New inventions, exploration and scientific discoveries".

In relation to scientific discoveries and advances those familiar with James Hannam's book *The Genesis of Science: How the Christian Middle Ages Launched the Scientific Revolution,* will appreciate how misleading the Oxford textbook is.

The negative portrayal of Christianity is made worse as the same kind of close scrutiny is not applied to other religions such as Islam. The description of Islam is matter of fact and ignores the often violent and destructive nature of jihad; the authors write, "caliphs, who succeeded Muhammad, continued to spread the Prophet's teachings throughout a growing Islamic empire". The statement that "The Ottoman Empire and Islamic faith spread from Asia into Africa and Europe, challenging the Christian belief system of medieval Europe" also implies that the process was benign.

No mention is made of practices such as dhimma where non-believers are denied the right to own property, are unfairly taxed and often live in fear of violence and expulsion from their communities and homes.

A third textbook published in 2010 and circulated to Australian schools titled *Learning From One Another: Bringing Muslim Perspectives into Australian Schools* continues to offer a misleading and one-sided view of Islam.

The textbook, on asking students to explain what they associate with the word *jihad* and after noting "there are no wrong answers", explains that it can refer to "spiritual struggle" as well as "armed fighting, often in self-defence".

An extract taken from *The Oxford Encyclopedia of the Islamic World, vol 2* is cited that claims the crusades and the "modern war on terror" are both motivated by "greed and scorn for Islam". The book also repeats the argument that the reason many Muslim nations are "socio-economically and educationally disadvantaged" is because of "former colonial powers".

Ignored is the counter argument that the fundamentalist interpretations of the Muslim religion, especially Sharia law, run counter to economic and scientific advancement and that the theocratic nature of Islam also restricts innovation and change.

Similar to the Oxford textbook the third textbook also presents the growth of Islam in a neutral way that ignores the violence, destruction and loss of freedom experienced by those living in the conquered lands.

The impact of expansion is described as follows, "many of the peoples of the newly conquered regions converted to Islam. Those who did not were allowed to live peacefully and practice their faith as long as they abided by the law of the land and paid the *jizya*, a tax imposed on non-Muslims".

Once again, there is no reference to the suffering, financial hardship and executions faced by those who wished to remain true to their religion.

Unlike secular critics who often attack non-denominational, Christian schools for teaching creationism and conservative views about reproduction and sexuality, the authors of the *Learning From One Another Textbook* counsel tolerance and respect for Islamic beliefs about such matters.

To point out that the above textbooks present a biased and simplistic view of religion, in particular Christianity and Islam, is not to argue against a full, objective and, where justified, critique of religion. Rather it is to argue that any such analysis should be fair and impartial.

In arguing for a more inclusive and comprehensive treatment of religion, especially Christianity, it is also important to distinguish between proselytising and educating students about religions and beliefs systems in a broader sense.

Christian values remain at the heart of our culture

There's no doubt the ABC when falsely accusing Christian men of being more prone to family violence is guilty of a cultural-left bias. And it's not just the ABC that's running a secular campaign against Christianity.

Read the Fairfax Press and the impression is that paedophilia mainly involves Catholic priests (ignored is that most children are abused by family or relatives), that Catholic schools don't deserve government funding and that there's no place for Christianity in public debates on issues such as abortion and euthanasia.

Academics such as historian Tony Taylor argue against including Judeo-Christianity in the school curriculum as it's a "Cold War rhetorical fiction" employed by "the Christian right".

In Victoria the Labor government has replaced religious instruction with its gender-free, anti-male Respectful Relationships program.

While secular critics are happy to undermine Christianity, especially Catholicism, what is ignored is Judeo-Christianity is central to Australia's cultural, economic, moral and spiritual wellbeing and one of the foundation stones of Western civilisation.

As argued by English poet TS Eliot in *Notes Towards The Definition of Culture*, Christianity is central to Western cultures when deciding right and wrong, the common good and how we should live our lives.

Eliot even says "if Christianity goes, the whole of our culture goes". The atheist Douglas Murray also argues about the importance of Christianity when he describes himself as a "cultural Christian".

Murray made the point in a debate with another atheist, Richard Dawkins, that in banishing religion the danger is people end up with "meaningless lives in a meaningless universe".

Given the rise of Islamic fundamentalism and the dramatic increase in Muslim migrants in Europe and England, Murray also argues it's vital "left-wing liberal progressives" recognise they are living "in the wake of the Judaeo-Christian tradition".

Evidence Eliot and Murray are correct includes the fact that concepts such as the sanctity of life, free will, being charitable to others and the separation between church and state are primarily Christian in origin.

Many of the most evil crimes against humanity have been committed by secular, godless ideologies such as fascism and communism. Hitler's gas chambers, Mao's starvation and torture of millions and Pol Pot's killing fields highlight the danger of denying the significance of religion, especially Christianity.

It's also important to recognise the benefits of Christianity to Australia's economic and social wellbeing. Catholic and other faith-based schools teach 34% of Australian students, saving Commonwealth, state and territory governments the billions of dollars needed if those students enrolled in government schools.

Christian schools, compared to most government schools, achieve stronger Year 12 results and are better at addressing bullying caused by racism, and parents see such schools as having more disciplined classrooms.

Christian-inspired or managed hospitals, philanthropic organisations and charities such as the Salvation Army, Catholic Health Australia, the Brotherhood of St Laurence and World Vision Australia are also integral part of Australia's health and welfare system.

Instead of presenting a negative and one-sided picture, secular critics such as the ABC and the Fairfax Press should acknowledge the benefits of Christianity and its central place in the life of the nation.

Let's not deny our Christian roots

Civil Liberties Australia, in its submission to the Senate inquiry on freedom of religion, argues Australia is not a Christian country on the basis that "it is not correct in law and in fact is directly contradicted by the Constitution".

The reality proves otherwise: although Australia is a secular society, where there is a division between church and state, to deny the significance of Christianity is to deny the nation's heritage and culture and to ignore what underpins our political and legal systems.

Rather than ignoring Christianity, the Constitution's pre-amble includes the words: "Humbly relying on the blessing of Almighty God" and parliaments around Australia begin with the Lord's Prayer.

Perth lawyer Augusto Zimmermann says Australia's political and legal systems owe much to Christianity.

He says: "It is evident the foundations of the Australian nation, and its laws, have discernible Christian-philosophical roots."

Concepts such as free will, the sanctity of life and a com-mitment to the common good are very much influenced by the New Testament. The admonition "Thou shalt love thy neigh-bour as thyself", while not always adhered to, underpins civility, tolerance and respect for others.

While a commitment to natural justice and liberty owes much to the Enlightenment, as argued by Larry Siedentop in *Inventing the Individual*, equally influential is the Bible's state-ment, "There is neither Jew nor Greek, there is neither bond nor free, there is neither male nor female: for ye are all one in Christ Jesus."

Christian charity and God's commandment to serve others also helps explain why Christian-inspired or Christian-managed health, education, welfare and charitable groups and organisations are an essential part of Australia's social fabric.

As TS Eliot contends in *Notes Towards a Definition of Culture*, to deny Christianity is also to deny much of the art, literature and music that Australia has inherited from Western civilisation.

Whether Bach's Mass in B minor, Faure's Requiem, or Handel's *Messiah*, the reality is that music's debt to Christianity is beyond doubt. Add Leonardo da Vinci's *The Last Supper*, Michelangelo's Sistine Chapel ceiling and Botticelli's *Virgin and Child with Two Angels,* and it's clear our culture owes a great deal to Christianity.

If it is true that most country and rural towns in Australia have a war memorial then it is also true that each will also have a church or place of worship.

And it is also true that Christmas and Easter, while increasingly secular in nature, are still predominantly religious celebrations that are central to our way of life.

Even though the percentage of Australians identifying as Christian has declined through the years, there is no doubt that Christianity is still the major religion. Based on the 2011 census figures, about 61% of Australians identified as Christians, with Muslims at 2.2%, Buddhists 2.5% and Hindus 1.3%.

Given the threat of Islamic terrorism in 2015, David Cameron as prime minister described Britain as a Christian nation, saying: "Yes, we are a nation that embraces, welcomes and accepts all faiths and none, but we are still a Christian country." The same can be said for Australia.

At the same time cultural-left groups such as Civil Liberties Australia seek to deny the nation's Christian heritage, they argue we must acknowledge indigenous cultural beliefs and history — but if the latter must be respected and recognised, so must the former.

Barnaby Joyce right that Australian values are based on Judeo-Christian principles

Thank you Barnaby Joyce — at least there is one senior member of the Federal Government ready and willing to identify what underpins our culture and what makes Australia unique.

While Prime Minister Malcolm Turnbull obfuscates about what constitutes Australian values and our way of life, the leader of the National Party is clear when arguing we are a Judeo-Christian nation.

Yes, the Prime Minister is right to identify values such as a commitment to democracy, human rights and freedom of conscience and freedom of speech but left unanswered is what underpins such values and beliefs and why so many other nations reject them.

China, Vietnam, Burma, Cambodia and Lao PDR are one-party states ruled by totalitarian regimes, where the freedoms and rights we take for granted are non-existent.

As argued by Ayaan Hirsi Ali in her book Heretic, Islam — unlike Western liberal democracies such as Australia — is a theocracy where the imams and the religion rule and there is no division between church and state.

Ali also argues that fundamentalist Islam is not a religion of peace — as demonstrated in Muslim terrorism — and that in countries such as Saudi Arabia, Iran and Brunei women and homosexuals are harassed and intimidated as official policy.

While the Australian historian Tony Taylor argues that Judeo-Christianity "simply does not exist" and that it is an example of "Cold War Christian rhetoric", the reality is that our parliaments begin with the Lord's Prayer and the Constitution includes the words "humbly relying on the blessings of Almighty God".

As detailed in Larry Siedentop's book Inventing the Individual: The Origins of Western Liberalism, it is also true that the New Testament, in particular, influenced the growth of liberalism and what the American Declaration terms "unalienable rights".

Such rights, including the right to "life, liberty and the pursuit of happiness", are described as "endowed by their Creator" and it should not surprise that the US's currency includes the words "In God we trust".

Equally as important as Judeo-Christianity when defining Western civilisation is the concept of natural law that can be traced back through Europe, Britain to ancient Rome and Greece.

The Roman philosopher Cicero describes natural law as "right and natural, commanding people to fulfil their obligations and prohibiting and deterring them from doing wrong. Its validity is universal; it is immutable and eternal".

Unlike the secular law imposed by dictators, oligarchs and other self-serving political elites, natural law is superior.

Cicero defines natural law as "right reason in accord with nature" and the US-based Jesuit philosopher Professor Joseph Koterski, argues natural law is central to providing a "universal standard of morality".

It should not surprise the US-based Freedom House puts Western liberal democracies such as Australia, England,

America and New Zealand at the top of the list when ranking countries in terms of democratic freedoms, values and institutions.

And the reality is that not all cultures are equal and millions around the world live under oppressive dictators.

Communist regimes such as Russia, Cuba, North Korea and China promise a workers' paradise based on the dictum "from each according to his ability, to each according to his needs".

But best illustrated by George Orwell's Animal Farm the promise of liberation is soon replaced by inequality, oppression, famine and misery.

Proven by the millions imprisoned in Stalin's gulags, the millions starved as a result of Mao's Great Leap Forward and Pol Pot's killing fields, Marxism is a failed and corrupt ideology.

As detailed in Robert Reilly's The Closing of the Muslim Mind it is also true that some cultures are not as evolved as Western civilisation. While we experienced the Renaissance, the Reformation and the Enlightenment, Islam never evolved and adapted in the same way.

Advocates of multiculturalism, where diversity and difference reign supreme and all cultures are considered worthy of respect, ignore the fact that the values on which multiculturalism is based are unique to Australia and other Western cultures.

Tolerance, respect and the right to life, liberty and the pursuit of happiness do not arise in a vacuum or by accident. The political and legal institutions that protect our way of life are also historically grounded in Western civilisation.

At a time when Australia is facing enemies and threats — both external and domestic — and when the nation is acknowledging the thousands that fought, suffered and died under the Australian flag, it is only right that we celebrate and defend what makes us unique.

Let's celebrate the role of Christianity in our culture

Proven by the celebration of Easter, while we are a secular society, we are also a culture deeply influenced by Christianity and the Bible.

TS Eliot, the English poet whose work inspired the musical *Cats*, argues Christianity underpins much of Western civilisation, including our legal and political systems, the concept of public and private morality and our literature and the arts.

When detailing what makes Western culture unique, Eliot argues: "It is against a background of Christianity that all our thought has significance", and goes as far as arguing, "if Christianity goes, the whole of our culture goes".

Whereas Muslim cultures worship the Koran, Hindus the Vedas, Buddhists the Sutras and Jews the Torah, the foundation text for Western culture is the story of Christ detailed in the Bible.

The English language, especially our literature, owes much to the Bible, especially the New Testament. Expressions like "turn the other cheek", "be a good Samaritan", "let he who is without sin cast the first stone", "the blind leading the blind" and "pride comes before the fall" are all derived from the Bible.

Literary texts like *The Canterbury Tales*, *Pilgrims Progress*, Dante's *Divine Comedy* and more modern examples like the *Narnia* books by CS Lewis, Patrick White's *Voss* and Tim Winton's *Cloudstreet* cannot be fully appreciated without knowledge of Christian beliefs and values.

Western art, proven by Michelangelo's Pieta and the Sistine Chapel and Leonardo da Vinci's The Last Supper and the Annunciation, draws heavily on Biblical references. Famous and enduring composers like Handel, Bach, Beethoven and Faure, in the same way, were inspired by Christian teachings.

The American Declaration of Independence describes the right to "Life, Liberty and the pursuit of Happiness" as God-given and it's no accident that banknotes are printed with the phrase "In God We Trust".

Zimmerman writes: "It is evident that the foundations of the Australian nation, and its laws, have discernible Christian-philosophical roots" and this explains why the Preamble to the Australian Constitution includes the words "humbly relying on the blessing of Almighty God".

The Biblical statement that "There is neither Jew nor Greek, there is neither bond nor free, there is neither male nor female: for ye are all one in Christ Jesus" forms the basis for Western legal and political concepts like the inherent dignity of each person and the right to freedom and liberty.

In a world where millions are denied the freedoms we take for granted, the fact that Australia is a Western liberal democracy heavily influenced by Christianity explains why so many migrants want to immigrate here and lead a free life.

The belief that we are made in God's image explains the value our culture places on the sanctity of life and the commandment to "Love thy neighbour as thyself" is the reason so many charitable and philanthropic organisations are Christian.

According to some estimates nearly 50% of Australia's health, education, social welfare and charitable organisations are either Christian or Christian in origin. With schools, for example, more than 20% of Australian students are taught in Catholic schools.

Julia Gillard when prime minister, and even though an atheist, stressed the value of the Bible when she argued it "formed such an important part of our culture" and that "it is impossible to understand Western literature without that key of understanding the Bible stories and how Western literature builds on them".

With home invasions, domestic violence, car thefts, street violence and robberies on the increase it's clear that many in society lack a moral compass and while the Bible is not the sole arbiter of what constitutes right and wrong, it represents an essential place to start.

Given the threat of Islamic terrorism and the way extremists use the Koran to justify their jihad against the West, it is even more vital that we acknowledge how the Bible underpins our way of life.

The 200th anniversary of the Bible Society of Australia was celebrated in 2017 and there is no doubt the Bible has had, and continues to have, a significant impact on our way of life.

Counteroffensive on the Western Front

There's no doubt that Western liberal democracies such as Australia, the UK, France, Germany and the United States are under attack. In Melbourne and Sydney Islamic extremists have killed innocents, and the Islamization of the UK and Europe is leading to ethnic ghettos and home-grown terrorism.

Given such threats, the decision to establish a foundation to champion Western civilisation, funded by a bequest from the late entrepreneur Paul Ramsay and chaired by John Howard, is significant and timely.

As I argue in *The Culture of Freedom* whether it is the enemy within, preaching political correctness, identity politics and victimhood, or the enemy without, represented by Islamic terrorism, our way of life is facing an existential threat.

The traditional academic curriculum has been replaced by a rainbow alliance of radical Neo-Marxist, postmodern and gender theories in which Cardinal Newman's ideal of an education championing "freedom, equitableness, calmness, moderation, and wisdom" is condemned as elitist, inequitable and obsolete,

As noted by the American academic Christopher Lasch, universities are no longer committed to independent critical inquiry "as it is no longer necessary to argue with opponents on intellectual grounds or to enter into their point of view. It is enough to dismiss them as Eurocentric, racist, sexist, homophobic — in other words as politically suspect".

In 2017 American students at Middlebury College in Vermont violently disrupted a speech by Charles Murray, an academic who argues that genetics play a powerful role in academic performance, chanting "Racist, sexist, anti-gay, Charles Murray go away!"

In England a report by the Adam Smith Institute based on the fact that "50% of the general public supports right-wing or conservative parties compared to 12% of academics" concludes "individuals with left-wing and liberal views are overrepresented in British academia".

Australian universities, with the occasional exception, are not immune. In his 1996 Boyer Lecture the ANU academic Pierre Ryckmans bemoaned how universities had also been captured by the cultural-left. After noting one incident where a young academic attacked a speaker, describing him as elitist and bourgeois for daring to make judgements of relative value and worth, Ryckmans concludes "to deny the existence of objective values is to deprive the university of its spiritual means of operation".

John Carroll from LaTrobe University details how the cultural-left uses "neo-Marxist categories of exploitation and oppression to find 'victims' of their own country's mendacity — so Australia becomes racist, cruel to refugees, misogynist, homophobic and increasingly riven by inequality. The tropes endure, with Islam the current exploited and oppressed repository of virtue".

The school curriculum has also been captured and is being used to promote identity politics and cultural relativism. Students are told they must embrace diversity and difference and that all cultures must be equally acknowledged and celebrated.

Except when it comes to Asian and Indigenous cultures that are given priority at the expense of Western civilisation — especially Judeo-Christianity, where in subjects like history, literature, art and music its treatment is scanty and superficial.

As noted by the literary expert Barry Spurr, the result is that while students get to study the contribution of Indigenous Australians there is little, if any, recognition of the central importance of the Western literary canon.

Greg Melleuish, from the University of Wollongong, is also critical when he argues that the history curriculum does not give enough "importance to the place of Western civilisation in world history, especially over the past two hundred years".

At the very time Western, liberal democracies are being undermined from within they are also being threatened by Islamic fundamentalism, best represented by Islamic State. Extreme interpretations of the Koran, as detailed by Ayaan Hirsi Ali in The Heretic, are committed to destroying Western nations by establishing an Islamic caliphate and sponsoring acts of terrorism.

Incidents like 9/11, the Bali bombings, the attack on the office of the satirical magazine Charlie Hebdo, the subsequent 2015 attacks in Paris and the genocide against Coptic Christians in Egypt represent a concerted campaign to destroy what the Koran describes as "the unbelievers".

While the overwhelming majority of Muslims are peaceful and law abiding it is also true that there are elements of the Koran that are hostile to our way of life. Fundamentalist Islam denies women the freedoms and liberties we take for granted and there is no division between church and state.

Unlike Western civilisation, where Christianity and historical movements such as the Reformation and the Enlightenment have led to the freedoms and liberties we now take for granted, Islam is not as accommodating.

Proven by Islamic terrorism and the cultural-left's political correctness movement there is much to be done to strengthen and defend Western civilisation against enemies foreign and domestic and the establishment of the Ramsay Foundation provides a beacon of hope.

It is right to teach religion in school like any other subject

The Queensland Government's decision to review Religious Instruction material in government schools highlights the issue of the place of religion, especially Christianity, in the curriculum.

One side of the argument is that government schools are secular in nature and there is no place for Religious Instruction or programs like the Commonwealth government's school Chaplaincy program.

In 2016 in Victoria, for example, the Andrews government removed Religious Instruction from the formal school curriculum by restricting it to lunchtime or before or after school.

Another example relates to Queensland's Ron Williams who challenged the Commonwealth Government's School Chaplaincy program in the High Court on the basis that governments did not have the right to fund religious programs in secular state schools.

The other side of the argument supports including religion in government schools as education, by its very nature, involves students learning about and acknowledging the importance of moral and spiritual values.

The Melbourne Declaration provides a policy road map that all Australian education ministers have endorsed and, when defining what constitutes a worthwhile curriculum, it refers to "moral and spiritual" values and the need for students "to understand the spiritual, moral and aesthetic dimensions of life".

The body responsible for the national curriculum being implemented by all states and territories, the Australian Curriculum Assessment and Reporting Authority, also stresses the importance of encouraging students "to learn about different religions, spiritualities and ethical beliefs".

It's also true that while state and territory based legislation stops government schools endorsing a particular religion or faith schools are allowed to include religion in the curriculum.

The Western Australian legislation states that it is permissible to include "general religious education in the curriculum of schools" and the Victorian education act allows teaching about "the major forms of religious thought and expression characteristic of Australian society and the rest of the world".

In NSW, similar to the Queensland legislation, the government allows state schools to allocate time "for the religious education of children of any religious persuasion". Whether described as Religious Education or Religious Instruction or part of the general curriculum, it is clear that teaching about religion is allowed.

While all accept there is no place for proselytising in government schools the arguments in favour of teaching about religion are manifest.

In an increasingly materialistic and narcissistic world where rates of bullying, self-harm, depression and youth suicide are on the increase it's clear that students need a strong moral compass based on sound ethical and moral values.

While not all religions are the same, the great religions of the world embrace the golden rule, do unto others as you would have them do unto you, and moral codes like the ten commandments provide a succinct guide about what constitutes right and wrong behaviour

Familiarity with Christianity is especially important as much of Western culture and what makes Australia unique can only be fully understood by learning about the significance and impact of the Bible; especially the New Testament.

Parliaments around Australia, with the exception of the ACT, begin with the Lord's Prayer and the Preamble to the Australian Constitution includes the words "humbly relying on the blessing of Almighty God".

The Perth based academic, Augusto Zimmerman, argues that much of English common law that Australia has inherited and seminal documents like the Magna Carta are underpinned by Christian values such as the sanctity of life, free will and a commitment to the common good.

Unlike Islam, which is a theocratic religion, the words from the Bible "Render therefore unto Caesar the things which are Caesar's; and unto God the things that are God's" explains why in liberal democracies like Australia there is a separation between Church and state.

And it should not surprise that the English atheist Richard Dawkins claims "A native speaker of English who has never read a word of the King James Bible is verging on the barbarian".

Much of Western literature and many of our daily expressions and sayings like 'turn the other cheek', 'the blind leading the blind, 'can a leopard change its spots?' and 'cast the first stone' draw on the Bible.

Ask whether Aboriginal and Torres Strait Islander spiritual and religious beliefs should be taught in schools and the answer is a resounding 'yes'. The great religions of the world, especially Christianity, deserve no less.

We must never forget the good work of Christianity

There's no doubt that it's a hard time being a Christian, especially if you are a Catholic. As Cardinal Pell admitted during his interview with Andrew Bolt many in the Church failed to confront the evil of child abuse and what happened destroyed the lives of hundreds of innocent and vulnerable children.

Add the fact that secular critics like Richard Dawkins and Christopher Hitchens argue believing in God is infantile and faith equals superstition and it's understandable why some, like Elise Elliot, turn their back on the Church (*Herald Sun* 24 February 2016).

I was also raised as a Catholic but, unlike Elliot, I have not forsaken the Church and what Christianity and the Bible offer.

Growing up in working class Broadmeadows during the '60s wasn't easy and having an alcoholic, violent father didn't make things any better. But, mother's faith, Mass on Sunday and prayer provided solace and the belief that there is good in the world.

Each night, before sleep, I would recite "Now I lay me down to sleep, I pray the Lord my soul to keep and if I die before I wake I pray to God my soul to take" and prayed that life would not always be so painful and difficult.

The Bible taught me that there is evil in human nature and that we are all open to temptation and sin but, at the same time the parables taught me about goodness, sacrificing oneself for others, redemption and the importance of having courage and being resilient.

Parables like the Good Samaritan and the Prodigal Son describe in a succinct and direct way important moral lessons like always helping others. Expression like 'turn the other cheek' and 'let him whom is without sin cast the first stone' helped me understand human nature and the importance of forgiveness.

Communion and confirmation at St Dominic's in Camp Road gave me a sense of belonging to something more significant and lasting by opening a transcendent world of ritual, mystery and faith.

And for those who believe that science dispels mystery and faith Albert Einstein writes "The fairest thing we can experience is the mysterious. It is the fundamental emotion that stands at the cradle of true art and true science…. It was the experience of mystery — even with mixed with fear — that engendered religion… in this sense, and in this alone, I am a deeply religious man".

There's no doubt that to be human is to suffer good and evil, joy and pain and love and loss. And for a parent there is no greater tragedy than losing a son or daughter. Such was the case when our son, James, was killed in a hit and run while walking home from a mate's party.

And again, it is religion that I turned to. Faith provides the belief that there is a world beyond this one and offers comfort and the hope that all is not lost.

The Christian mystic, Julian of Norwich, also points to an essential truth when she writes "But we cannot escape the suffering and the sorrow: there are dark sides to life. Realism forces us to face the fact. And the same realism enables us to trust the light and life and love in which we are enfolded".

While nothing will ever erase the suffering and pain of losing a son religion and the words of Christian mystics like Julian of Norwich provide solace and a sense that we are all a part of something larger and beneficial.

No one can deny the fact that there are evil priests who victimised and destroyed the lives of innocent children and young men and women. At the same time, it is vital to acknowledge the profound an ongoing debt owed to Christianity and the Church.

Catholic schools across Australia enrol 20% of students, charitable organisations like the Salvation Army and World Vision help millions of the poor and disadvantaged both here and overseas.

Whether health, medicine, social welfare or helping those who are victims of domestic violence or drug abuse it is Christian groups and bodies like Compassion Australia and the St Vincent de Paul Society that underpin Australia's social services and welfare sector and without which governments would be unable to cope.

The English poet and mystic William Blake, while no defender of organised religion, argues "He who sees the Infinite in all things sees God. He who sees the Ratio only sees himself only".

Elliot concludes her piece by writing "And I won't open the heavy doors of church ever again". For me that is not an option. It is by opening the doors that we enter a rich, spiritual world that transcends the present and offers balm to a weary soul.

January 26 is Australia Day.
Stop trying to change it.

WITH Australia Day approaching it's a good time to ask: what does it mean to be Australian? One answer is that we are a multicultural society where diversity and difference prevail and, as a result, there is no such thing as an Australian.

Those advocating multiculturalism argue we are a nation of ethnic and racial groups each with its own unique way of life. Instead of being Aussies we are Italian-Australian, Greek-Australian, Lebanese-Australian, Irish-Australian, Anglo-Australian or Vietnamese-Australian.

That because we are a land of immigrants with different languages, customs, religions and beliefs that are all considered equally worthwhile it's also wrong to argue that there is a mainstream Australian culture that binds everyone together.

Reality check — the first thing to understand is that if we only focus on what divides us then we will become a nation of tribes.

As noted in the Australian Bureau of Statistics Australian Social Trends, April 2013, and notwithstanding the propaganda about being cosmopolitan, there is such a thing as the average Australian.

The ABS survey states "despite the considerable diversity in Australia and the changes Australia has gone through over the years, the largest group of Australians have actually changed very little".

Christianity is still the major religion at 61%, while the number professing Buddhism is 2.5%, Islam 2.2% and Hinduism 1.3%. Despite the high rate of migration, it is also true that "the average Australian was born in Australia and so were both parents".

Ninety per cent of those who reported their ancestry described themselves as English, Australian, Irish or Scottish. Add the fact that our political and legal institutions are inherited from the UK and it should not surprise that we are a Western, liberal democracy where basic rights are guaranteed and all are free to live their lives without state intervention and control.

Australians are egalitarian, down to earth and practical, and we value heroism and self-sacrifice. This explains why, according to the US-based Freedom House, while Australia has one of the highest ratings for protecting freedom, countries in our region such as China, Thailand, Myanmar, Lao PDR, Vietnam and Cambodia are categorised as totalitarian.

Our culture, according to the Freedom House, guarantees freedom of speech and a free media while such rights are denied in the majority of countries in Africa, Asia and the Middle East.

As anyone who has travelled overseas will appreciate, there is a uniquely Australian culture and one that distinguishes us from the rest of the world. Compared to the Brits and Americans Australians are egalitarian, down to earth and practical.

When chauffeured Australian politicians travel in the front next to the driver, we treat our bosses as equals and millions of migrants have been welcomed on the basis that we believe in a "fair go". With sporting heroes such as Shane Warne and comedians such as Paul Hogan it's clear that Australians like larrikins and, as shown by Sam Kekovich's lamb ads, we have a unique sense of humour.

Only Australia could have produced Dame Edna and her gladioli. With sporting heroes like Shane Warne (left with Indian cricketer Sachin Tendulkar) and comedians like Paul Hogan it's clear that Australians like larrikins.

The fact that the description "mate" can be used both as a term of endearment or an insult is uniquely Australian, as when it is employed to cover the fact that you can't remember the name of the person you are talking to.

Proven by the thousands travelling to the shores of Gallipoli every year and those walking the Kokoda Track, it's also true Australians value heroism and self-sacrifice and that patriotism is alive and well, especially among our young.

As described by Dorothea Mackellar's poem *My Country* and evidenced by weather events in Sydney and many parts of inland Australia, we are a land of "droughts and flooding plains". Our climate and terrain are unique and help fashion who we are.

It's true that migrants have changed our way of life — compared to 40 years ago cafes and espresso coffee are mainstream, wine has nearly outstripped beer as the beverage of choice and Asian-rim cooking is widespread.

At the same time, regardless of ethnicity, religion or race, we are all Australian with a unique culture that all should acknowledge and celebrate.

Why the West is best

US academic Samuel P. Huntington, after the end of the Cold War and the collapse of the USSR, argued that the new global conflict would be between cultures when he said: "The great divisions among humankind and the dominating source of conflict will be cultural."

Based on the rise of Islamic fundamentalism and Islamic State's reign of terror in Africa and the Middle East and in

London, Paris, New York, Boston, Melbourne and Sydney, it's clear how prescient Huntington was.

Globally, Western liberal democracies like Australia and the values and way of life we take for granted are under attack, both in terms of physical terror and violence and the fear that we are no longer safe.

As noted by the human rights activist born in Somalia and raised as a Muslim, Ayaan Hirsi Ali, Islamic fundamentalism strikes at the heart of Western beliefs like the sanctity of life, individual liberty, and freedom of religion, association and press that so many have fought for and died to defend.

In her book, *Heretic*, Hirsi Ali argues "Islam is not a religion of peace" and that Islamic terrorists use the Koran to justify their jihad against the West and the practice of killing or converting unbelievers.

The fact Islam is a theocratic religion where there is no division between church and state and where sharia law prevails provides additional evidence that in Western cultures like Australia the liberties and freedoms we take for granted are threatened. That Western culture is under attack is made worse by the fact that there is also an enemy within.

Since the cultural revolution of the mid-to-late-'60s — the time of the Paris student riots, Vietnam War moratoriums, Woodstock and flower power — the cultural-left has embarked on the long march to weaken Western culture.

During the '60s and '70s students on American campuses chanted "Hey-hey, ho-ho, Western Civ has got to go!" and the great works of the Western literary canon and the belief that Western culture made the world a better and safer place were all deconstructed and critiqued.

Australian universities also suffered, as noted by Pierre Ryckmans in his 1996 Boyer Lectures. Ryckmans argued that undergraduates were no longer culturally literate and universities were no longer true to the ideal of the disinterested pursuit of knowledge, wisdom and truth associated with the vision articulated by Cardinal Newman.

Best illustrated by the mistaken concept of multiculturalism, where the argument is that all cultures are equal and that it is wrong to impose Western, liberal beliefs and values, the tenor of the times is one of cultural relativism.

Worse still, many of the cultural-left, instead of defending the very culture that ensures their freedom, argue the West is inherently destructive, inequitable and unjust. Marxists argue capitalism is based on greed; ecowarriors that our lifestyle is destroying the environment; and feminists that society is misogynist and patriarchal.

However, the reality proves otherwise. History proves that Western culture is pre-eminent in defending what the American Declaration of Independence refers to as "life, liberty and the pursuit of happiness".

Christian concepts such as the sanctity of life, the separation of church and state, a commitment to the common good and social justice ensure that our freedoms and rights are sustained.

Our Westminster parliamentary system, legal institutions and common law also distinguish Western culture from those, like Islamic State, that are barbaric, totalitarian and riven with self-serving ambition and power.

It's no coincidence that the American-based Freedom House gives higher rankings to Western nations such as America, England, New Zealand and Australia for protecting civil liberties and political rights compared to countries like China, Thailand, Myanmar, Lao PDR, Vietnam, Cambodia and Russia.

Science, technology and reason, beginning with the Ancient Greek philosophers and brought to fruition with the

Enlightenment and the Industrial Revolution, are also unique products of Western culture.

Scientific reasoning and technology allow planes to safely take off and land, bridges to stay upright, and for the world's population to experience record levels of health and wellbeing.

While many on the cultural-left yearn for the socialist utopia, from each according to his abilities and to each according to his needs, the truth is as proven by Orwell's *Animal Farm* that capitalism is far superior.

Capitalism, based on risk-taking and the ability to make a profit, leads to innovation and growth in areas like technology and science. As argued by Friedrich Hayek in the Road to Serfdom, capitalism, by embracing subsidiarity, also acts against centralised and oppressive state control.

Instead of denigrating and undermining Western culture we should acknowledge and celebrate what we have achieved.

Discounting Christianity in our schools denies history

With schools opening and students about to return education is in the news. While school funding, academic standards and teacher quality are perennial issues equally as vital is what is being taught in the school curriculum.

And when it comes to the curriculum one of the burning issues both here and overseas is the place of religion in the school day.

In his Christmas speech, former British prime minister, David Cameron, declared that Britain is a "Christian country" and the Education Secretary, Nicky Morgan, has ordered schools to teach that "the religious traditions of Great Britain are, in the main, Christian".

Closer to home, the NSW government argues that Special Religious Instruction classes are an essential part of the normal school curriculum and, unlike in Victoria, classes will not be banished to lunchtime or before and after school.

The Andrews government, on the other hand, instead of recognising our Christian heritage is pushing a secular, anti-Christian agenda. Evidence includes taking Special Religious Instruction classes out of the school timetable.

Further evidence is the decision to ban Christmas hymns that acknowledge the birth of Christ during the normal school day. While secular Christmas decorations and carols are permitted in state schools what is described as "praise music (that) glorifies god or a particular religious figure or deity regardless of music style" cannot be part of a normal school activity.

While allowing secular Christmas carols like Rudolf the Red Nosed Reindeer the ban stops students from singing religious hymns except in Special Religious Instruction classes.

The only problem is that Special Religious Instruction classes are no longer part of the normal school timetable.

The instructions to principals also state that while schools can "put up Christmas decorations or pictures of Santa" that "religious material cannot be displayed or distributed in schools or on school grounds" — effectively banning nativity scenes.

No doubt the same restrictions that apply to Christmas will also apply to Easter.

The Australian National Curriculum, which Victorian schools have to teach, is also secular in nature and religion, especially Christianity, is once again ignored and undermined.

In history students are told at every year level that they must learn about Aboriginal and Torres Strait Islander culture, customs and spiritual values and beliefs but there are only one or two references to Christianity.

The Civics and Citizenship curriculum, when detailing the vital contribution charitable, community and philanthropic groups make to society, makes no mention of the Brotherhood of St Lawrence, St Vincent De Paul or the Salvation Army.

Even though Christianity is a central part of Australia's history and culture the argument is that we are a multicultural, secular society and that religion is irrelevant.

Ignored is that Australia is a Western, liberal democracy where concepts like the sanctity of life, free will, truth telling and individual rights and freedoms are largely based on the Bible, especially the New Testament.

It's no surprise that the Preamble to the Australian Constitution includes the words "Humbly relying on the blessing of Almighty God" and that parliaments around Australia begin with the Lord's Prayer.

The Perth based academic Augusto Zimmermann argues "Judeo-Christian values were so embedded in Australia so as to necessitate the recognition of God in the nation's founding document... it is evident that the foundations of the Australian nation, and its laws, have discernible Christian-philosophical roots".

And, as detailed by the Tasmanian author, David Daintree in his book *Soul of the West: Christianity and the Great Tradition*, the reality is that Western art, literature and music are also influenced by Christianity.

Classic stories like *The Pilgrim's Progress*, *The Canterbury Tales*, Dante's *Inferno* and more classics like C S Lewis' *The Chronicles of Narnia* and novels by Patrick White have a strong Christian influence.

Michelangelo's Sistine Chapel, da Vinci's The Last Supper and music like Handel's Messiah and songs like Amazing Grace only exist and have meaning because of Christianity and the Bible.

The Australian Education Union argues that "public education is secular" and that there must be "freedom from religion in teaching programs". What the Union ignores is that the Victorian legislation clearly states that government schools are allowed to teach "about the major forms of religious thought and expression characteristic of Australian society and other societies in the world".

The Melbourne Declaration is the policy document endorsed by all education ministers and it also argues for including religion in all schools when it states that a balanced education must teach moral, spiritual and aesthetic beliefs and values.

While it's true that Australia is a secular society where there is a division between church and state the reality is that we, like Britain, are a Christian nation where religion underpins much of who and what we are.

We need to teach our kids that West is best

Former prime minister Tony Abbott is correct to argue there is a link between terrorism and Islam and more needs to be done to defend and promote the benefits of Western civilisation.

For far too long multicultural apologists have refused to make the connection and to call on Islamic leaders to confront the fact that extreme forms of Islam are barbaric, anti-Western and evil.

Abbott is in good company. David Cameron, when the British Prime Minister, also argues there is a link between terrorism and Islamic fundamentalism.

After arguing that Britain is a Western, liberal, democratic country that owes much to its Christian heritage and ongoing traditions David Cameron states: "Denying any connection between the religion of Islam and the extremists doesn't work ... it is an exercise in futility."

Cameron also warns that those in the media and universities who refuse to criticise Islamic fundamentalism because they "look the other way through a mixture of misguided liberalism and cultural sensitivity" must name Islamic-inspired terrorism for what it is, instead of being politically correct.

Abbott is also right to argue aspects of the Koran are ossified and obsolete because, as also argued by the Somalian activist Ayaan Hirsi Ali, Islam has never experienced epochal events such as the Renaissance, the Reformation and the Enlightenment.

As a result, Islam is a theocratic religion, women and homo-sexuals are denied equal rights and those who fail to conform or criticise are condemned as apostates to violence and death.

Proven by the rise of Islamic state and Boko Haram it is also clear, as detailed in Mark Durie's book *The Third Choice*, that the jihad against the West only leaves three options to unbe-lievers: Conversion, death, or subjugation and loss of freedom.

Abbott is also correct to argue not all cultures are equal. For all its faults Western civilisation is unique and a far better alternative to oppressive cultures where individual freedoms and liberties are denied.

Because of Christian- inspired concepts like sanctity of life, free will, a commitment to the common good and the need to "love thy neighbour as thyself" we are able to go about our daily lives free of violence and coercion.

The admonition "There is neither Jew nor Greek, there is neither bond nor free, there is neither male nor female: for ye are all one in Christ Jesus" suggests all must be treated fairly and it is wrong to discriminate without good reason.

The secular concept of natural law that can be traced to ancient Rome and the philosopher and orator Cicero also helps define Western culture as unique and worth safeguarding.

Cicero argued that "the safety of citizens, the preservation of states, and the tranquillity and happiness of human life" is a universal truth that must be upheld regardless of personal or religious belief.

The statement in the American Declaration of Independence that "We hold these truths to be self-evident, that all men are created equal, that they are endowed by their Creator with certain unalienable Rights, that among these are Life, Liberty and the pursuit of Happiness" embodies a commitment to natural law.

What's to be done? The Australian Chinese scholar Pierre Ryckmans argues: "You cannot usefully approach a foreign culture, specifically a rich and sophisticated foreign culture, if you do not have a firm grasp of your own culture."

Ryckmans also argues that instead of our schools and universities giving students a comprehensive and balanced understanding and appreciation of Australian culture and the debt owed to Western civilisation, cultural relativism and political correctness prevail.

Cultural-left academics argue there is nothing unique or preferable about Western culture, that we are a secular society that owes nothing to Christianity and that young Muslims are radicalised because they are victimised and oppressed by mainstream society.

A number of submissions to the review of the national curriculum, that I co-chaired, also argue that focusing too much on Asian, indigenous and environmental priorities ignores the fact that we are a Western, liberal democratic country where Christianity is the dominant religion.

By privileging cultural diversity and difference, the new code for multiculturalism, the criticism is also made that students are being given a sanitised version of Islam while Christianity is either ignored or presented as oppressive, violent and Eurocentric.

Ayaan Hirsi Ali argues that winning the battle against Islamic terrorism cannot simply rely on physical force.

Equally as important is inculcating "into the hearts and minds of young people an ideology of life, love, peace and tolerance". The very attributes that make Western civilisation unique.

A prayer to protect our heritage

Should daily sessions of the Victorian Parliament, as they currently do, begin with the Lord's Prayer? The practice is a well-established part of the Westminster parliamentary process that we have inherited from Britain and, with the exception of the ACT, is carried out in all state, territory and commonwealth parliaments.

The Victorian Greens Party's Ellen Sandell argues 'no' because she believes the practice is obsolete and no longer suitable because Victoria is a multicultural, multi-faith society.

Wrong. While we are a multicultural, multi-faith community Christianity is the major religion both in terms of numbers and also in relation to the contribution it has made and continues to make to our way of life and political and legal institutions.

As argued by the Liberal member for Kew, Tim Smith, when criticising the Greens MP for not attending the opening session when the Lord's Prayer is recited, it "exhibits a total lack of respect and almost contempt for the ancient traditions of this House".

The Tasmanian Liberal Senator, Eric Abetz, when the Greens tried to remove the Lord's Prayer from the Commonwealth parliament, makes a similar argument when he says that the Lord's Prayer "is a very rich part of our cultural tradition and a humble acknowledgement by the Parliament collectively of its responsibilities".

At the time of Federation 92% of Australians described themselves as Christian and, while the figure has fallen, based on the 2011 census 58% of Victorians still describe themselves as Christian.

With Buddhism at 3.1%, Islam 2.9%, Hinduism 1.6%, Judaism 0.8% and other religions 0.9% it is clear that Christians constitute the majority of those Victorians willing to express a religious conviction.

While we are a secular society where there is a clear division between the Church and the state, it is also true that we are a Western, liberal democracy where Christianity plays a central role in our culture and how society operates.

Our political and legal systems are based on Christian principles like the sanctity of life, not lying under oath and having free will and being responsible for one's actions. It should not surprise that the Preamble to the Australian Constitution includes the phrase "humbly relying on the blessing of Almighty God".

Democratic principles that we now take for granted and that guarantee our freedom, like governments not being above the law and all citizens being entitled to fair, impartial and timely justice, can be traced back to Britain and Magna Carta that celebrated its 800th anniversary in 2015.

As argued by the legal expert Dr Zimmermann from Murdoch University in a speech to the Tasmanian Parliament, the Magna Carta "is first and foremost a religious document that underlies the biblical justification for limited government under law".

Zimmermann also argues the concept of common law that Australia has inherited from Britain and that underpins our legal system owes its origins to Christianity.

He writes, "common law owes much to the influence of Christian natural law theory. This legal system was originated and largely influenced by the moral convictions of lawyers, philosophers and politicians who believed in the existence of a higher law reflecting enduring principles of freedom, justice and morality".

The fact that Victoria and Australia are Western liberal democracies where Christianity has such a significant influence explains why so many millions of immigrants leave their countries to settle here.

Unlike totalitarian and oppressive regimes like North Korea, Iran, Saudi Arabia and Cuba our rights are protected and we are free to go about our business without fear or favour.

The example of Islamic state, where Christians are beheaded, Muslim women are brutalised and raped and homosexuals killed proves how fortunate we are and why we must protect and celebrate what makes our way of life unique.

And it's not just our political and legal systems to which Christianity has contributed. Philanthropic and charitable organisations like the Salvation Army and the Brotherhood of St Laurence serve the underprivileged and disadvantaged.

Christian organisations like Baptcare and the St Vincent de Paul Society also contribute to the Victorian community by providing aged care facilities plus much needed support and help for those who are victims of domestic violence and alcohol and drug abuse.

When it comes to education it is also the case that Christian schools, especially Catholic schools that enrol the majority of students, save the government millions of dollars every year as such schools receive less funding than government schools.

It's ironic that while progressive, left of centre politicians like Ellen Sandell are the first to argue we must protect indigenous culture, spirituality and traditions when it comes to Christianity, one of the bedrocks of Western civilisation, they argue nothing needs to be acknowledged, safeguarded and preserved.

Christianity is central to Western values and culture

As noted by American academic Samuel P. Huntington 20 years ago, the "great divisions among humankind and the dominating source of conflict will be cultural".

One need only observe the ongoing conflict between extremist versions of Islam and Western culture to see the truth of Huntington's observation. Given the prevalence of what he describes as "the clash of civilisations" the question that must be addressed is: what makes Western civilisation unique and what aspects of our culture are most worth defending?

One response argues that there is nothing unique or special about Western culture. Those committed to multiculturalism and diversity and difference suggest Western culture is made up of various influences and traditions.

Australia, for example, since 1788 has embraced immigrants from around the world, each with their own customs, habits, beliefs and way of life that are acknowledged and celebrated.

In its more extreme form those advocating multiculturalism adopt a relativistic stance where all cultures are considered of equal worth and those seeking to champion Western civilisation are criticised for being Eurocentric, binary, patriarchal, elitist and reactionary.

The result, as detailed in Allan Bloom's *The Closing of the American Mind*, is the death of rigorous and balanced academic studies in the liberal-humanist tradition.

As argued by La Trobe University's John Carroll in *Quadrant*, the cultural-left's view of Western culture is one where "art has to be shocking; values have to be deconstructed; meanings have to be exposed as rationalisations for entrenched privilege and wealth".

A second response, as detailed by Pierre Ryckmans in his 1996 Boyer Lectures, is to argue that while particular cultures may be variegated it is important to recognise that cultures also have unique and distinctive characteristics.

Ryckmans argues that cultures are "indivisible" and that it is impossible to understand a foreign culture from a Western perspective "if you do not have a firm grasp of your own". In relation to teaching about China, Ryckmans asks: "How can you explain the influence of Nietzsche upon Lu Xun to students who have never read Nietzsche?"

T.S. Eliot in *Notes Towards a Definition of Culture* also argues that while Western culture has drawn on a range of other influences there are "common features" that identify the many nations that are heirs to the Western tradition, and central to Western culture is Christianity.

Eliot writes, "To our Christian heritage we owe many things beside religious faith. Through it we trace the evolution of our arts, through it we have our conception of Roman Law which has done so much to shape the Western world, through it we have our conceptions of private and public morality."

While there is no doubt that philosophy, reason and the scientific method of testing truth claims traced to the Enlightenment and back further to ancient Greece have had a profound impact on Western culture it is equally true Judeo-Christianity has had a significant and enduring influence.

As argued by American academic Thomas E. Woods, "Western civilisation stands indebted to the church for the university system, charitable work, international law, the sciences, important legal principles and much else besides."

The fact Western cultures still celebrate Christmas and Easter and aphorisms such as "turn the other cheek", "let he among you without sin cast the first stone" and "render unto Caesar what is Caesar's" are still in use illustrate the impact of Christianity.

Biblical commandments such as "Thou shalt not kill", "Do not steal", "Do not bear false witness" and "Do not commit adultery" underpin much of the Western legal system, as do concepts such as the sanctity of life and the importance of absolution and redemption. Murdoch University's Augusto Zimmermann says: "The common law was heavily influenced by Christian philosophy. This philosophy argues that there is a divine reason for the existence of fundamental laws, and that such laws are superior to human-made legislation."

The evil nature of totalitarian regimes, such as communism and fascism, is that they are premised on the belief that man-made laws reign supreme, that power and violence instead of reason are the final arbiters and that utopia can be created on this earth.

While secular critics argue that faith and reason are antithetical to one another, it is also true Christian scholars and intellectuals have contributed in a significant way to Western culture's intellectual heritage.

Central to Cardinal John Henry Newman's concept of a university is the formation of a habit of mind that "lasts through life, of which the attributes are freedom, equitableness, calmness, moderation and wisdom". Although written more than 150 years ago, what Newman argues provides a healthy tonic to those who view education as simply about promoting productivity and economic competitiveness.

Christian philosophers such as St Thomas Aquinas, George Weigel argues in *The Cube and the Cathedral*, are central in providing "a bridge in European culture between the classical world and the medieval world (one that) yielded a rich, complex and deeply humanistic vision of the human person, human goods, human society and human destiny". Central to Aquinas's philosophy, Pope John Paul II stated in *Fides et Ratio*, is "the courage of the truth, a freedom of spirit in confronting new problems, the intellectual honesty of those who allow Christianity to be contaminated neither by secular philosophy nor by a prejudiced rejection of it".

Somali-born Dutch-American activist Ayaan Hirsi Ali, who writes extensively on the dangers of fundamentalist forms of Islam, argued in an interview on the ABC that to fight terrorism the West must "inculcate into the minds and hearts of young people an ideology or ideas of life, love, peace and tolerance".

While a military response and anti-terrorism strategies are vital, equally as important is the need to defend the values Hirsi

Ali refers to; values that are essential characteristics of Western, liberal democracies such as Australia.

SAFE SCHOOLS, SAME-SEX MARRIAGE AND THE LGBTQI SEXUALITY AND GENDER AGENDA

Marxism offers both the hope and the strategy needed to create a world where human sexuality, gender and how we relate to our bodies can blossom in extraordinary new and amazing ways that we can only imagine today... It is through a revitalised class struggle and revolutionary change that we can hope for the liberation of the LGBTI people.[3]

---

3   Roz Ward. 2015. Extract from a speech given at a 2015 Marxism conference, Melbourne.

The real agenda is for schools

Advocates of same-sex marriage, including senior members of the Turnbull Government Simon Birmingham and Christopher Pyne, argue that a 'yes' vote will not adversely impact on religious freedom and the right to follow the church's teachings.

Supporters of same-sex marriage also argue the issue is simply about marriage equality and not about promoting a radical, cultural-left gender and sexuality agenda. Wrong on both accounts.

Evidence from both here and overseas proves that if marriage is redefined to allow same-sex couples to marry then faith-based organisations, bodies and individuals will be penalised and made to suffer because of their religious convictions and beliefs.

In Victoria the owners of a holiday camp who refused to accommodate a gay/lesbian group were taken to court and financially penalised. In Tasmania an LGBTQI activist Martine Delaney lodged a complaint with the Anti-Discrimination Commissioner over the Catholic Church circulating the *Don't mess with marriage* booklet to schools.

Given that both the Australian Labor Party and the Greens Party are committed to removing existing exemptions and exceptions to anti-discrimination laws relating to the ability to discriminate based on religious grounds then it's obvious that religious freedom will be under even greater threat if the definition of marriage is changed.

Overseas examples include a British Christian school having its performance downgraded as the Ofsted inspectors concluded it was "homophobic" as it failed to teach the officially endorsed, secular view of LGBTQI diversity and difference.

In London a Jewish school enrolling girls aged 3 to 8 was threatened with closure for not teaching the government's endorsed beliefs about gender fluidity and gender reassignment.

In America, under the Obama administration, schools were forced to allow transgender boys to use girls' toilets and changing rooms. If the same-sex legislation is passed the reality is that schools in Australia will also be forced to implement a radical LGBTQI sexuality and gender agenda.

The Australian Education Union, one of the most powerful teacher unions in Australia, in addition to supporting same-sex marriage argues that "Homosexuality and bisexuality need to be normalised" in the school curriculum and that "All staff must be in-serviced in homophobia and hetero-sexism".

The AEU policy for schools also argues it is wrong to believe that heterosexual relationships are "natural" or "normal" and condemns churches as "un-Christian" for not accepting its cultural-left LGBTQI agenda.

It is also the case that the cultural-left has long sought to undermine Christianity and to banish religion from the public square and that the same-sex issue is part of a much broader campaign.

As argued by Aubrey Perry in a comment piece published in the Fairfax Press in August 2017 titled *This survey is about much more than same sex marriage*, the intention is to enforce a secular view of society, one where religion plays no part.

In relation to the SSM postal survey Perry argues: "This survey offers us a conscious opportunity to make a firm stand in support of a secular government and to reject discrimination or favouritism based on religion. It's our opportunity to say that religion has no part in the shaping of our laws".

The ALP senator Penny Wong, in her Frank Walker Memorial Lecture, also suggests that there is no place for religion in law making when she argues "The separation of church and state is one of the central planks on which liberal democracy stands".

In relation to issues like same-sex marriage Wong argues "The problem in all of this, of course, is the application of religious belief to the framing of law in a secular society". If religion has no place one wonders why parliaments begin with the Lord's Prayer and why the Constitution includes the words, "Humbly relying on the blessing of Almighty God".

Roz Ward, the La Trobe University researcher responsible for the radical LGBTQI Safe Schools program that tells children gender is fluid and limitless, goes one step further and argues there is no place for a religious view of marriage as "only Marxism provides the theory and practice of genuine human liberation".

Ward goes on to argue "Marxism offers both the hope and the strategy needed to create a world where human sexuality, gender and how we relate to our bodies can blossom in extraordinary new and amazing ways that we can only try to imagine today".

Underpinning the campaign to change the definition of marriage is a radical LGBTQI gender ideology, described by Pope Francis as one "which denies the difference and reciprocity in nature of a man and a woman and that envisages a society without gender differences, thereby removing the anthropological foundation of the family".

The Pope also argues that defining marriage as involving people of the same-sex "leads to educational programmes and legislative guidelines which promote a personal identity and emotional intimacy radically separated from the biological difference between male and female".

Church values threatened

One of the myths associated with the same-sex marriage debate is the argument that redefining marriage will not have any adverse impact on the church and those faith-based organisations and individuals committed to a religious view of marriage that involves a woman and a man.

At the time of writing, faith-based bodies, like schools, are exempted from anti-discrimination laws in relation to who they employ and who they enrol. Such exemptions are justified by national and international covenants and agreements guaranteeing the right to freedom of religious beliefs.

Faith based schools, compared to government schools, also have greater freedom in relation to whether or not to implement radical, Marxist inspired gender fluidity programs like Safe Schools and Respectful Relationships.

If the definition of marriage is changed, based on what is happening overseas and also the stated policies of the Australian Education Union, the Australian Labor Party and the Greens Party, then there is no doubt that existing freedoms will be lost.

In the UK, as noted by the University of Worcester's Institute of Education, religious schools are no longer free to follow their beliefs as they "are bound by the Equality Act 2010, the Public Sector Equality Duty and the Teachers' Standards in the same way as non-faith schools, with the same legal requirements for equality, inclusivity and the tackling of bullying".

As a result, after the then Cameron Government implemented a program to make all schools teach British values, a Christian school was criticised as "homophobic" and its performance downgraded as the inspectors felt it failed to teach the officially endorsed, secular view of LGBTQI diversity and difference.

A Jewish school in London teaching girls aged 3 to 8 was threatened with closure for not teaching the government endorsed beliefs about gender fluidity and gender reassignment. Additional evidence that religious freedom is being lost in the UK is a statement by the head of a review into integration where she condemns Catholic schools that follow the church's teachings as "homophobic and anti-gay marriage".

A second myth surrounding the same-sex marriage debate is that religion has no role to play as Australia is a secular society and long gone are the days when Christianity was a vital part of our social fabric.

Wrong. While it's true that the numbers are declining based on the 2016 census the reality is that 60% of the population describe themselves as religious with the majority being Christian.

And while it's true that not all attend church it's also equally true that the majority of Australians base their moral values on Christian beliefs like the sanctity of life, love thy neighbour as thyself and doing good rather than evil.

Visit most country towns across Australia and along with a pub and memorial to those who have fallen in battle there's no doubt that there will also be a place of worship. And it should not surprise that in moments of national tragedy like the Bali bombings and the shooting down of Flight MH17 that we turn to prayer and church services to lessen the sorrow and pain.

While pro-SSM advocates argue that our parliaments are secular it's also true that the political and legal freedoms we take for granted owe a significant debt to Christian beliefs, moral and values.

That's why parliaments begin with the Lord's prayer and why the preamble to our constitution includes the words "humbly relying on the blessing of Almighty God". As argued by Larry Siedentop in *Inventing the Individual: The Origins of Western Liberalism* many of the freedoms we enjoy draw heavily on the Bible, especially the New Testament.

The admonition "There is neither Jew nor Greek, there is neither slave nor free, there is neither male nor female; for you are all in in Christ Jesus" underpins the belief in what the American Declaration of Independence describes as the "unalienable rights" to life, liberty and the pursuit of happiness.

While there's no doubt that Christians and the church are guilty of committing great crimes and sins it is also true that religion contains within itself the ability to distinguish right from wrong and to better protect the rights of the individual.

Those primarily responsible for abolishing slavery in England and across the then British Empire were Christians and the overwhelming majority of Australia's charitable, health, educational and welfare organisations and bodies are either Christian in origin or Christian managed and owned.

As argued by Douglas Murray, the author of *The Strange Death of Europe: Immigration, Identity, Islam*, the reality is that to deny the importance of Christianity is to deny one of Western civilisation's foundation stones and weaken and undermine what makes nations like Australia so special and so unique.

Left wants to banish religion from our lives

The heading to Aubrey Perry's comment piece in yesterday's Fairfax press ("This survey is about much more than same-sex marriage") reveals the true intent behind the cultural-left's campaign to redefine the definition of marriage.

Forget minister Simon Birmingham's argument that changing the Marriage Act is simply about saying Yes or No. Saying Yes will radically undermine the place of religion in Australian society and deny the individual's right to religious freedom.

Perry, like many in the LGBTQI community committed to Marxist-inspired gender and sexuality theories, argues the central issue related to same-sex marriage is about "the shaping of our country and future freedoms, an acceptance or denial of religion steering our public policymaking and governing our legislative body".

Perry sees no place for religion when she argues, "This survey offers us a conscious opportunity to make a firm stand in support of a secular government and to reject discrimination or favouritism based on religion. It's our opportunity to say that religion has no part in the shaping of our laws".

While many Australians genuinely believe that gay people should be allowed to marry, it's also obvious that the cultural-left's agenda is to banish religion from the public square and to enforce a secular world view devoid of religious belief and faith.

The gender and sexuality policies advocated by the ALP and the Greens best illustrate the cultural-left's intention to enforce a secular agenda on religious organisations, schools and charities — who, at the time of writing, were exempted under existing anti-discrimination laws.

The Greens argue, "All people have fundamental human rights and are entitled to equal protection of the law without any discrimination, including on the basis of sexual orientation, gender identity or intersex status".

The ALP's policy states it will "strengthen laws and expand programs against discrimination and harassment on the basis of sexual orientation, gender identity and intersex status".

Whether faith-based aged care, health, education, hospitals or schools, the ALP's and the Greens' policies are clearly aimed at restricting freedom of religion. One only needs to look at overseas examples to see what will occur if the ALP and the Greens are successful.

One of the arguments employed to justify same-sex marriage is that Australia is a secular society where religion no longer has any importance or significance. Not so. While it is true that Australia is a secular society, the reality is that our legal and political institutions owe much to Judeo-Christianity.

As detailed in Douglas Murray's book, *The Strange Death of Europe,* it is impossible to deny the historical and ongoing influence of Christianity on Western civilisations such as Australia.

Perry concludes by arguing that a Yes vote will move "us toward a government free from religious influence and discrimination". As Murray notes, based on examples of secular ideologies like fascism, communism and postmodernism, to deny religion does not always lead to a better world.

The glaring problems with same-sex marriage

There are a number of reasons why many Australians are against same-sex marriage — ranging from religious beliefs to secular arguments and the fact, ignored by those pushing the 'yes' vote, that there are those within the LGBTQI community not interested in marriage as they prefer a less restrictive lifestyle.

Listen to those advocating same-sex marriage and the overwhelming impression is that the LGBTQI community fully supports the proposed change. The public is told again and again that gays and lesbians, in particular, are clamouring to validate their relationships by being entitled to marry in the same way heterosexual couples are.

The ALP's Bill Shorten and Penny Wong as well as Liberal gay activists like Tim Wilson base much of their argument in favour of same-sex marriage on the assumption that it is widely accepted by the gay and lesbian community.

Not true as the evidence suggests there are many within the LGBTQI community who are either opposed to getting married or do not see it as beneficial or worthwhile. Jessica Merritt on Sydney's Heaps Gay website describes the push for same-sex marriage as "myopic" and argues "Equality isn't an issue that the community itself is united on".

Drawing on the publication *Against Equality: Queer Critiques of Gay Marriage* Merritt notes many LGBTQI people oppose same-sex marriage as it is "essentially conservative" and that it represents an "unnecessary validation of a relationship that is authentic in its own right".

Merritt also notes that those in a same-sex relationship are already protected under Australia's civil law and that the debate about same-sex marriage has been high jacked by "self-appointed leaders" guilty of imposing "heteronormative equivalency" on the LGBTQI community.

Two national surveys, *Private Lives A Report on the Health and Wellbeing of GLBTI Australians* and *Monopoly, Monopoly? Polygamy? A Study of Gay Men's Relationships 2014* provide additional evidence that not all within the LGBTQI community want to be married.

The first survey notes "Only a very small percentage of men

and women (between 5-10%) reported formalising the relationship with a marriage or commitment ceremony, while most others had no wish to do so".

The second survey, dealing principally with gay men, concludes "Few men had experienced any public relationship ceremony, and only a minority expressed a clear interest in marrying their primary regular partner".

And contrary to the arguments put by the same-sex marriage lobby that there are a multitude of Australians who are gay and lesbian a national survey carried out by La Trobe University puts the figure at less than 2% with 98% of Australians identifying as heterosexual.

Those advocating a change to the marriage act to include same-sex couples, in addition to ignoring the fact that many within the LGBTQI community are happy to lead a more open and promiscuous lifestyle, ignore the true meaning of marriage.

Not surprisingly, as marriage between a women and man is one of the foundation stones of Western culture, the Shorter Oxford dictionary defines marriage as "the action, or an act, of marrying: the ceremony by which two persons are made husband and wife".

The dictionary also describes a wedding as becoming "the husband or wife of (a person) by participating in a prescribed ceremony or formal act". For hundreds of years across all the major religions and cultures the reality is that marriage has always involved a man and a woman.

The fact that marriage involves a man and a woman for the purpose of procreation where children, overwhelmingly, are raised by their biological parents also suggests that while gay and lesbian couples can have a loving and sincere relationship their union is not a marriage as defined.

No amount of wishful thinking can deny the reality is that conceiving a child requires a man and a woman and that explains why gay and lesbian couples have to rely on a third person if they are to have a child.

As argued by the American College of Pediatricians, "human sexuality is an objective biological trait" and "Human sexuality is binary by design with the obvious purpose being the reproduction and flourishing of our species". Something that gay and lesbian couples are unable to achieve.

And it should be noted that while gays and lesbians are not able to be married they receive the same rights as de-facto couples in terms of superannuation and other financial and legal affairs. It's also true that long gone are the days when gays and lesbians suffered injustice and were discriminated against.

Events like the AFL's Gay Pride match, the number of corporations advocating gay and lesbian rights such as Qantas and the major banks and the prevalence of gay and lesbian relationships in mainstream movies and TV shows how society is now more tolerant and open.

As argued by Sydney's Catholic Archbishop, Anthony Fisher, there is also the real and present danger that if same-sex marriage is legalised then religious organisations and individuals committed to the Church's teaching will suffer discrimination and injustice.

Gay liberals cry 'look at us!'

The Western Australian Liberal Senator Dean Smith supports gay and lesbian marriage on the basis that "there are so many wanting to get married". Another liberal politician Trent Zimmerman also supports gay and lesbian marriage when arguing it's wrong to "deny the right of all Australians to be married".

Other same-sex marriage supporters such as the Australian Labor Party's Bill Shorten and Penny Wong also want the Australian public to believe that gays and lesbians are desperate to be married in the same way heterosexual couples are.

Wrong. As they say never let the facts get in the way of a good argument. The reality is that the majority of lesbian, gay, bisexual, transgender, queer or questioning, and intersex (LGBTQI) people are not committed to a long-term, monogamous relationship symbolised by the institution of marriage.

Based on two national surveys, *Private Lives: A report on the health and wellbeing of GLBTI Australians* and *Monopoly a Study of Gay Men's Relationships,* it's obvious that a significant number of LGBTQI people prefer a more fluid and transient lifestyle.

The first survey concludes "Only a small percentage of men and women (between 5-10%) reported formalising the relationship with a marriage or commitment ceremony, while most others had no wish to do so".

The survey also notes "It is of interest that the majority of respondents between (52% of men and 39% of women) indicated no intention or wish to formalise their current relationship".

The second survey reaches a similar conclusion when it states, "only a minority of men indicated they would like to marry their primary regular partner". With men with multiple partners, as might be expected, the percentage answering 'yes' to the question 'Would you marry partner' sits at 11%.

It's ironic that while Smith, Zimmerman, Shorten and Wong argue in favour of same-sex marriage that many in the LGBTQI community, apart from a few radicalised individuals, show no real interest and, in fact, prefer a more promiscuous lifestyle.

In addition to same-sex marriage advocates mistakenly arguing that gays and lesbians want to embrace traditional marriage they argue that any public debate associated with a plebiscite will lead to public attacks against the LGBTQI community causing anxiety and distress.

The leader of the ALP Bill Shorten goes as far as implying any debate will lead to gays and lesbians committing suicide. Penny Wong argues "I oppose a plebiscite because I don't want my relationship — my family — to be subject of inquiry, of censure, of condemnation, by others".

Ignored is that it has been the advocates of same-sex marriage that have been the most offensive. Bill Shorten when arguing against a plebiscite stated "I don't want to give haters a chance to come out from under the rock and make life harder for LGBTQI people or their families".

Katherine Hudson the co-founder of the LGBTQI advocacy group Wear It Purple has compared advocates of heterosexual marriage to "dictators, despots and despicable leaders, including Putin, Kim Jong-un, Mugabe and ISIS terrorists".

One only needs to remember the storm of protest against Australia's tennis legend Margaret Court after she argued against same-sex marriage to see where the real bias and prejudice lie.

Liberal politicians like Smith and Zimmerman also oppose a plebiscite on the basis that a public debate will lead to open displays of hostility. Ignored is that Australia, with the odd exception, is a mature, civil society and that the majority of voters are able to debate issues sensibly and in a balanced way.

Also ignored is that while we are a parliamentary democracy where our elected politicians decide policies on our behalf sovereignty lies with the people. Voters are sick of politicians failing to keep their promises and there's no doubt that the Turnbull Government was elected on the promise that the people would decide the marriage issue.

Read and listen to the advocates of same-sex marriage and the impression is that a significant number of Australians are LGBTQI and that heterosexuality is no longer the norm.

The Safe Schools program being implemented in schools, for example, argues that about 15% of students are LGBTQI and that gender is fluid and limitless. As a result, marriage should no longer simply involve a man and a woman.

The truth is that approximately 98% of Australians identify as heterosexual and only a small percentage of the 2% that are LGBTQI express a desire to embrace the traditional view of marriage — one that by definition involves a male and a female for the purpose of procreation.

It is also true that even without being formally married same-sex couples have the same legal rights as heterosexuals couples in areas like superannuation and related financial affairs.

Nothing safe in ignoring basics in education

Parents have every right to be worried about the LGBTQI Safe Schools gender and sexuality program being forced on government schools by the Daniel Andrews government.

Add the fact, as reported in the *Australian*, that vulnerable teenagers with intellectual disabilities enrolled in Victorian special schools are also being indoctrinated and it's understandable why so many now call the program Un-Safe Schools.

Such was the furore about Safe Schools indoctrinating students with a Marxist inspired curriculum, where gender is fluid and limitless and boys can be girls and girls can be boys, that the Commonwealth censored the program and cut its funding.

Not so in Victoria where the uncensored version is being promoted and the education minister, James Merlino, is quoted as saying "Work is underway on expanding Safe Schools to all Victorian government schools by the end of 2018".

Supporters argue the program is about anti-bullying and making schools a safer place for students — wrong. Roz Ward, the Marxist academic responsible for designing the program, publicly admits its real purpose is to impose a radical, alternative view about gender and sexuality.

Ward states, "Safe Schools Coalition is about supporting gender and sexual diversity, not about stopping bullying". She says it's about "sexual diversity, about same sex attraction, about being transgender, about being lesbian, gay, bisexual — say the words transgender, intersex".

And just because the ALP government severed its ties with Roz Ward and La Trobe University's Research Centre in Sex, Health and Society in 2016 doesn't change the fact that the Safe Schools material is still guilty of advocating an extreme, cultural-left view of gender and sexuality.

One of the recommended resources, *OMG I'M Queer*, notwithstanding approximately 98% of Australians identify a heterosexual and are comfortable being men and women, tells students that "sexuality can't really be defined".

The statement is made that "sexuality is fluid, and changes over time" and "Looking at sexuality as something that's fluid and always changing is pretty cool".

According to Safe Schools "What you label yourself is up to you" as "Common definitions of sexuality, gender and sex are often limited" and because gender and sexuality "exist on a spectrum rather than absolute binaries".

Ignored, as argued by the American College of Pediatricians and with very rare exceptions, is that we are all born with either 'XY' or 'XX' chromosomes and "Human sexuality is binary by design with the obvious purpose being the reproduction and flourishing of our species".

Even though most children are happy being boys or girls the Safe Schools material argues "Gender isn't quite as simple as whether you're 'male' or 'female'. Everyone has their own gender identity in relation to masculinity or femininity".

Victoria's version of Safe Schools also repeats the misleading statistics used by the LGBTQI lobby when justifying the need for government funding and positive discrimination.

The *All of Us* booklet tells students that 10% of people are same-sex attracted. Ignored is one of the largest Australian surveys titled *Sexual identity and practices*, by Anthony Smith and Paul Badcock, that concludes only 1.6% on men identify as gay and 0.8% of women as lesbian.

On reading the Safe Schools material on the Victorian Department of Education and Training's website parents are left in no doubt that Safe Schools is more about LGBTQI advocacy than stopping bullying.

Schools are told that language should be gender neutral and, as a result, "Phrases like 'ladies and gentlemen' or 'boys and girls' should be avoided".

Schools are also told they should ensure, regardless of whether students are male and female, that they should be able to use "the toilets, changing rooms, showers and swimming facilities based on the student's gender identity and the facilities they feel most comfortable with".

Victoria's Safe Schools program is not the only alternative, cultural-left program being forced on schools. The Respectful Relationships material is also one-sided and biased.

Even though the Victorian Royal Commission concluded that 25% of family violence involves men as victims the Respectful Relationships program implies it's only women who are at risk. Boys and men are portrayed as misogynist and inherently violent.

Once again gender is presented as a social construct that is impossible to define because whatever gender you are is "determined by what an individual feels and does, and how individuals understand their identities including being a man, women, transgender, gender queer and many other gender positions".

The scandal is that at the same time the Andrews government is forcing a politically correct gender and sexuality program on government schools we are going backwards in international literacy and numeracy tests — now ranked 24th in the Progress in International Reading Literacy Study. So much for the basics.

Full Marx how ideology infiltrated schools

What parents have to realise is there is nothing new or unusual about the controversy surrounding the allegation that Sydney's Cheltenham Girls' High has banned gender specific terms such as girls and boys in favour of gender-neutral language.

A second example of adopting a lesbian, gay, bisexual, trans-gender, queer or questioning, and intersex (LGBTQI) agenda is Newtown High School of the Performing Arts allowing students to wear either the girls' or boys' uniform regardless of gender. Add the furore surrounding the lesbian-inspired Gayby Baby film being shown in schools and the Safe Schools Coalition program and it's clear that there is a concerted campaign by LGBTQI advocates to force their radical agenda on schools.

And those enforcing a cultural-left agenda on students, like La Trobe University's Roz Ward, responsible for the Safe Schools program, make no secret of the ideology underpinning their long march through the education system.

In a speech at the 2015 Marxism Conference, Ward argues, "LGBTI oppression and heteronormativity are woven into the fabric of capitalism" and "it will only be through a revitalised class struggle and revolutionary change that we can hope for the liberation of LGBTI people".

In the same speech, titled *The Role Of The Left For LGBTI Rights*, Ward goes on to argue "Marxism offers both the hope and the strategy needed to create a world where human sexuality, gender and how we relate to our bodies can blossom in extraordinary new and amazing ways that we can only try to imagine today".

Welcome to the world of gender theory. A world, as argued by the Gender Fairy story, where primary-school children can choose the gender they want to be as "only you know whether you are a boy or a girl. No one can tell you".

And it's been happening for years. As detailed in my 2004 book Why Our Schools Are Failing, cultural-left academics, the Australian Education Union and the Australian Association for the Teachers of English are long-term advocates of the LGBTQI agenda.

The 1995 AATE journal is dedicated to promoting a cultural-left view of gender and sexuality.

One paper calls on English teachers to explore "alternative versions of masculinity", while another warns against "the various ways in which gender categories are tied to an oppressive binary structure for organising the social and cultural practices of adolescent boys and girls."

The AEU's 2001 policy argues that either/or categories like male and female are not natural or normal and that "all curriculum must be written in non-heterosexist language".

The AEU's policy goes on to argue that any discussion about LGBTQI issues must "be positive in its approach" and "homosexuality and bisexuality need to normalised".

Ignored is that according to one of the largest national surveys of Australians, about 98% self-identify as heterosexual and babies, with the odd exception, are born with either male or female chromosomes.

Fast forward to the NSW's Teachers Federation's LGBTQI policies and it's clear little has changed. The Federation supports the Safe Schools program and anyone arguing for the primacy of male/female relationships is guilty of "heterosexism".

Anyone committed to the belief there are two genders is guilty of promoting "fear and hatred of lesbians and gay men" and the belief "other types of sexualities or gender identities are unhealthy, unnatural and a threat to society".

Ignored, compared to many other countries, including Saudi Arabia, Iran, Russia, India (where gay sex is illegal) and African nations such as Nigeria, Uganda and Zimbabwe, is that Australia is a tolerant and open society.

Football clubs have gay pride matches, many of our elite sports men and women have no problem "outing" themselves and the Gay/Lesbian Mardi Gras is widely accepted.

What LGBTQI advocates have to accept is parents are their children's primary teachers and caregivers and imposing a politically correct, radical LGBTQI agenda on schools is more about indoctrination than education.

What's so secret about Safe Schools?

The NSW Education Department is wrong to deny the FOI request to publicly identify those schools enrolled in the Safe Schools gender and sexuality program.

Parents have every right to know whether their child's school in involved and if the new Education Minister, Rob Stokes, is committed to openness and transparency then the names of schools must be made public.

After all, if the Western Australian, South Australian, Tasmanian and Northern Territory governments make the details public the same should apply to NSW. What has the Department got to hide?

Deciding where their children go to school it one of the most significant decisions parents make and it's only fair their decision is based on detailed information. Especially given the LGBTQI inspired program, reviewed by the NSW government, still advocates a radical, Marxist view of gender and sexuality that many parents find unacceptable.

One of the booklets is co-authored by La Trobe University's Roz Ward and she argues, "LGBTI oppression and heteronormativity are woven into the fabric of capitalism" and "It will only be through a revitalised class struggle and revolutionary change that we can hope for the liberation of LGBTI people".

The Safe Schools material argues there's nothing natural about being a boy or a girl. Students are told that they must "Define sexual diversity as a continuum" that "Everyone has their own identity in relation to masculinity and femininity".

Even though a national survey concludes approximately 98% of Australians identify as male or female and, according to the University of Sydney's Patrick Parkinson, only 1 to 3% are gay or lesbian, the Safe Schools material argues "around 10% of people are same sex attracted".

Research also proves while a minority of children and adolescents might experience uncertainty about their sexuality, what is described as 'gender dysphoria', the majority outgrow the condition over time.

The Safe Schools program ignores the research and tells vulnerable students that the condition is permanent.

The material also tells students that instead of sexual and gender identity being determined by whether you have 'XY' or 'XX' chromosomes that "it's up to the individual to describe what gender identity suits them best".

If a boy self-identifies as a girl schools are told that they should "confirm the toilets, changing rooms, showers and swimming facilities (are) based on the student's gender identity and the facilities they feel most comfortable with".

Ignored are the rights of the overwhelming majority of other students who are happy being boys and girls and whose parents expect schools to protect their privacy.

Further evidence that Safe Schools is about LGBTQI ideology rather than anti-bullying is how the program, similar to Big Brother in George Orwell's *Nineteen Eighty-Four*, uses language to indoctrinate students.

The 'Glossary and Inclusive language' describes students or parents who favour the more traditional view of gender and sexuality involving a man and a woman as guilty of "Heterosexism", "Homophobia", "Transphobia" and being "Heteronormative".

Ours is an age of identity politics and victimhood where the curriculum is awash with teaching students about the rights of politically correct minority groups. Instead of programs like Safe Schools indoctrinating students it's time to focus on what schools are meant to do — teach the basics.

Especially as over the last 4 to 8 years NSW students' literacy and numeracy results, measured by the national literacy and numeracy tests (NAPLAN), have gone backwards. It is also true that teaching about gender and sexuality is best left to parents as they are their children's primary care givers.

Do gays really want gay marriage?

The ALP's Bill Shorten and Penny Wong argue that we cannot have a plebiscite on marriage because the Australian people, supposedly, are homophobic, transphobic and heteronormative — as argued by the Marxist inspired Safe Schools Coalition material.

Both the ALP leader and senator also argue that marriage is one of the last obstacles to true liberation and equality and this explains why the LGBTQI community overwhelmingly endorses changing the Commonwealth's marriage act to include same-sex couples.

Wrong. The real reason is because Shorten and Wong are afraid that if the question of changing the marriage act is put to the Australian people sanity will prevail and the answer will be 'no'. Add the fact that a sizeable number of Australia's LGBTQI community are not interested in same-sex marriage and it's clear why the ALP want the decision made by Parliament.

Not only do many gays and lesbians prefer the freedom of multiple partners to a relationship "to the exclusion of all others, voluntarily entered into for life" but surveys also show that being able to marry is definitely not a priority.

Describing itself as one of the "largest surveys of gay, lesbian, bisexual, transgender and intersex (GLBTI) people ever conducted" the report titled *Private Lives: A report on the health and wellbeing of GLBTI Australians* concludes that marriage recognition is a very minor issue.

The report states "Only a small percentage of men and women (between 5-10%) reported formalising the relationship with a marriage or commitment ceremony, while most others had no wish to do so".

When discussing relationship status, the report also notes, "It is of interest that the majority of respondents between (52% of men and 39% of women) indicated no intention or wish to formalise their current relationship".

A second national survey, titled *Monopoly: A Study of Gay Men's Relationships* and involving 4,215 gay and bisexual online respondents plus face-to-face interviews, reports a similar conclusion in relation to gay men. Under the heading 'Marriage & Other Ceremonies' the survey states, "only a minority of men indicated they would like to marry their primary regular partner".

In relation to men with multiple partners, as might be expected, the percentage answering 'yes' to the question 'Would you marry partner' sits at 11%.

As to why marriage is not an important issue, the second survey goes on to suggest that one of the principal reasons is because a significant number of gay men are not committed to monogamous relationships.

In relation to gay men with a regular partner the second survey concludes, "only a third of the men described their relationship as monogamous" while the first survey notes "gay men are much more likely than the other groups to have known their most recent sexual partner for less than 24 hours".

While is it true that marriage between a man and a woman is not always monogamous or lasting, as previously stated those wishing to marry pledge themselves to a relationship "to the exclusion of all others, voluntarily entered into for life". The ideal is where two people commit themselves to one another in a lasting bond based on mutual trust and respect.

While an uncomfortable truth to some, it is also the case that marriage involves procreation; something denied in gay and lesbian relationships.

GLBTI school programs such as the Safe Schools Coalition and Victoria's Building Respectful Relationships, as they are seeking to normalise GLBTI relationships, present a positive image that fails to acknowledge the dangers and risks.

In relation to domestic violence the Private Lives survey reports that the incidence of partner abuse is "disturbingly high" and "the levels of experience of domestic violence represent a considerable burden of distress and injury for GLBTI people".

While concluding, "it is also clear that most GLBTI people live happy and fulfilled lives" the survey also notes that GLBTI people face unacceptable levels of discrimination and violence and high levels of anxiety and depression.

In relation to mental health, "Nearly three quarters of the sample reported some experience of depression in the past" and, even worse, "16% of all respondents indicated suicidal ideation (thoughts) in the two weeks prior to completing the survey".

While same-sex marriage is an issue at the top of the ALP's policy wish list, it is significant and revealing that those most affected by any change to the marriage act seem so little concerned or interested.

It's also the case, based on the two national surveys, that if Bill Shorten and Penny Wong are seriously committed to improving the life of LGBTQI people then they would address the issues that most impact on them, instead of wasting time, energy and resources on a politically correct, largely irrelevant campaign about marriage.

Marxist view of Australia a long way from the truth

It shouldn't surprise that La Trobe University's Roz Ward, one of the founders of the radical LGBTQI Safe Schools Coalition program, has been forced to resign from a Victorian government advisory role for calling the Australian flag "racist" and suggesting it should be replaced by a socialist inspired "red one".

Ward is a long-time member of Victoria's Socialist Alliance and a committed Marxist who believes that capitalism must be overthrown to make way for the workers' paradise.

Ward, when defending the controversial gender and sexuality program, argues: "LGBTI oppression and heteronormativity are woven into the fabric of capitalism" and "It will only be through a revitalised class struggle and revolutionary change that we can hope for the liberation of LGBTI people".

In the same speech titled *The Role of the Left for LGBTI Rights* and given at a 2015 Marxism Conference Ward argues "Marxism offers both the hope and the strategy needed to create a world where human sexuality, gender and how we relate to our bodies can blossom in extraordinary new and amazing ways that we can only try to imagine today".

The ALP leader Bill Shorten, in defending the program, is wrong to say it is about stopping bullying. One only needs to read Ward's justification for the Safe Schools program to find further evidence of her revolutionary zeal.

Ward admits, "Safe Schools Coalition is about supporting gender and sexual diversity, not about stopping bullying". She goes on to say it's about "sexual diversity, about same sex attraction, about being transgender, about being lesbian, gay, bisexual".

While advocates justify the Safe Schools program as an anti-bullying program the reality is that it is a Trojan horse employed by Marxist and socialist-left activists to force a radical lesbian, gay, bisexual, transgender, queer or questioning, and intersex (LGBTQI) agenda on innocent children and schools.

The Gender Fairy children's book tells kindergarten children that gender is fluid and limitless and that "Only you know whether you are a boy or a girl. No one can tell you". Activists argue that boys who self-identify as girls, regardless of their age, should be allowed to use girls' changing rooms and toilets.

One of the activities associates with Safe Schools, called *Freedom Fighters*, asks students to imagine the earth has been invaded by Martians and that the aliens reverse traditional gender roles and force girls to act as boys and boys to act as girls.

The students rebel and argue girls and boys can be whatever gender they want, singing: "You don't have to be a certain way just because you have a penis, you don't have to be a certain way just because you have a vagina". Apparently, gender is a social construct and your sexuality at birth has nothing to do with being a boy or a girl.

Another of the Safe Schools booklets claims that approximately 16% of students are LGBTQI. Ignored is that one of the largest surveys analysing sexuality and gender found that 97% of Australian men and women identify as heterosexual. Also ignored is a second survey that discovered only .05 to 1.0% of couples identify as same-sex.

No amount of Marxist wishful thinking and rhetoric from radical activists like Roz Ward can escape the fact that heterosexuality is the norm and that the overwhelming majority of Australians identify as being male or female.

Reading the Safe Schools Coalition material and the impression is that Australians are bigoted and biased as the majority of us, supposedly, are homophobic, transphobic and heteronormative.

Ignored is the reality that Australia is one of the most egalitarian and tolerant nations on earth. Survey suggest that the majority of Australians support same-sex marriage, the Sydney Gay/Lesbian Mardi Gras is mainstream and 800 companies and businesses are happy to publicly commit themselves to changing the Marriage Act.

Politicians like Bob Brown and Senator Penny Wong, business people like the CEO of Qantas Alan Joyce, sportsman like Ian Thorpe and the former Justice of the High Court Michael Kirby are all accepted and praised even though they are not heterosexual.

As a result of the controversy surrounding the Safe Schools Coalition gender and sexuality program it was reviewed by the Commonwealth Government. In response the Commonwealth education minister, Simon Birmingham, restricted it to secondary schools and the more extreme LGBTQI material and websites have been removed.

Instead of removing the offending aspects of the Safe Schools program Premier Daniel Andrews and the education minister, James Merlino, have decided to fully fund the program, to make the uncensored version compulsory for Victorian schools and to allow schools across Australia to access the Victorian Safe Schools website.

The rainbow blackboard

Did you know that Romeo and Juliet is to be condemned for 'promoting an oppressive binary structure for organising the social and cultural practices of adolescent boys and girls'? If not, thanks to Big Chalk's gender agenda, your kids sure will.

At the same time the Andrews government is removing religious instruction from the school curriculum there can be no doubt that it is pushing a radical cultural-left agenda about sexuality and gender on Victoria's school children.

This shouldn't surprise, as Premier Andrews is a key member of the ALP's Socialist-Left faction and Labor's policy, taken to the 2014 election, states an incoming government must "improve the health and safety of same-sex attracted and gender-questioning (SSAGQ) students by ensuring schools and health services effectively address homophobia, including content of sexuality education".

While all accept that bullying and unfair discrimination are wrong, the reality is that what Premier Andrews supports is more about advocating a radical lesbian, gay, bisexual, transgender, queer and intersex (LGBTQI) lifestyle than actually making schools safer.

The Andrew's government's Safe Schools Coalition program, while sold as an anti-bullying initiative, is more about indoctrinating children.

School children are told that gender is fluid and limitless, that they can decide what they want to be. *The Gender Fairy* storybook, designed for children as young as four, suggests being transgender is normal and it's OK not to identify as male or female.

The *Safe Schools Do Better* booklet tells students that about 16% of children are same-sex attracted, gender-diverse, trans- or intersex, even though a random survey of over 19,000 Australian men and women discovered that 98% identified as heterosexual.

Worse, children are taught that anyone who suggests "normal" relationships involve men and women are to be condemned as "heteronormative", "homophobic" and/or "transphobic".

Such are the concerns about the lack of objectivity and the fact that the Safe Schools material is not age appropriate that a review commissioned by the Commonwealth government called for significant changes.

These included schools needing to get parental approval before teaching the program, which is not to be used in primary schools, and giving parents the right to opt-out. As expected, in addition to making the Safe Schools program compulsory, Andrews has refused to have a word changed.

Another school program — Building Respectful Relationships — is also causing controversy. Part of the program asks students to read raunchy and provocative personal ads more suited to pornography sites and then to write their own (below, at left, is part of the teachers' lesson plan.

Parents, always their children's primary carers, need to realise that what is happening in Victoria is not new, that the cultural-left has been pushing its radical agenda on schools for years. The Australian Education Union is the largest and most powerful teacher union in Australia and its 2001 Policy on Gay,

Lesbian, Bisexual and Transgender People argues that "homosexuality and bisexuality need to be normalised" in the school curriculum.

The AEU also argues that it is wrong to believe heterosexual sex and relationships are "natural" or "normal", and it condemns churches as "un-Christian" if they do not agree with the radical LGBTQI agenda.

The AEU's 2003 policy goes further in demanding that "all staff must be in-serviced in homophobia and heterosexism" and "all curriculum must be written in non-heterosexist language". It is no surprise that "discussion of GLBT issues in a class situation should aim to be positive in its approach".

The Australian Association for the Teaching of English has also been a long-time supporter of a cultural-left view of gender and sexuality. In 1992 an academic in the English teachers' journal described traditional approaches to literature as "bourgeois, patriarchal, ethnocentric" and argued they needed to be deconstructed and exposed.

A second academic argued that the English classroom should be used to "elaborate alternative versions and styles of masculinity in attempting to move beyond an oppressive gender bind".

The belief is that traditional fairy tales like Cinderella and Snow White unfairly enforce a heterosexist view because the happy ending involves the heroine marrying the prince. Shakespeare's Romeo and Juliet and Jane Austen's Emma are also unsuitable, as they enforce "an oppressive binary structure for organising the social and cultural practices of adolescent boys and girls."

The Victorian curriculum is not alone in making schools enforce a radical view of sexuality and gender. The 2001, South Australia's curriculum, under the heading Gender Equity, argued that gender is a "social construct" and heterosexuality enforces unfair dominant power relations that must be deconstructed.

Parents might wonder why, at the same time the Andrews government wants to force its radical gender agenda on schools, it has banished religious instruction from the formal school curriculum. It's clear where the government's priorities lie. Instead of a strong moral compass, the focus is on advocating a radical LGBTQI secular agenda.

Criticising safe schools does not make you homophobic

In response to the Commonwealth's inquiry into the Safe Schools Coalition program Bill Shorten, the leader of the ALP, has labelled one of the program's main critics, Senator Bernardi, as a "homophobe";

Also, in relation to the Safe School's inquiry and Minister Birmingham's response to the report by William Louden a number of critics have attacked the Commonwealth Government for bowing to conservative Christians both inside and outside parliament.

The Green's Senator Robert Simms argues it is "clear that Malcolm Turnbull has thrown LGBTI young people under the bus today by bowing to the right-wing backbench bullies and stripping back the Safe Schools program".

Lucy Nicholas, from Swinburne University on the Conversation website, describes the members of parliament critical of the Safe School program as "white, cisgender, heterosexual male politicians" and the argues the proposed changes will lead to a situation where bullying LGBTQI students "is normalised".

Judged by the reaction to the proposed changes to the Safe Schools program one could be forgiven for believing that it is no longer available to schools. In fact, the opposite is the case as all schools will be able to access the program and its official website and in Victoria the state government has signalled the program will be mandatory for government schools.

While it is the case that the Commonwealth Government has restricted third party access to the Safe Schools Coalition website, given the nature of the Internet, there is nothing to stop schools, teachers, and students, for that matter, accessing what might be considered controversial sites like Minus 18 that advocate a LGBTQI sexual and gender agenda.

Critics of the changes, like Lucy Nichols, argue it is wrong to require parental approval before schools implement the program and that it is also wrong to give parents the right to withdraw their children from LGBTQI classes.

Ignored is the reality that parents are their children's first teachers and that the *International Covenant on Civil and Political Rights* argues that parents are primarily responsible for the children's moral education.

The Covenant states: "The States Parties to the present Covenant undertake to have respect for the liberty of parents and, when applicable, legal guardians to ensure the religious and moral education of their children in conformity with their own convictions (Article 18, point 4).

It is reasonable and fair that if parents are able to withdraw their children from Religious Instruction classes, on the ground that they disagree with their children learning about religion, then parents should also be able to opt out of the Safe Schools program.

This is especially the case given that some of the resources and materials associated with the Safe Schools Coalition program and website are controversial and most likely questionable given the age of the children involved.

The 'The Gender Fairy' story where primary school children as young as 4 years old are told "Only you know whether you are a boy or a girl. No one can tell you" provides one example.

Another example is the *gQ gender Questioning* booklet that asserts that "There are many genders beyond just 'male' and 'female'; gender can be fluid and limitless" and that Trans people can be "lesbian, gay, bisexual, queer, straight or something else".

Ignored, according to research carried out by Anthony Smith and Paul Badcock from La Trobe University is that out of the 10,173 men and 9, 134 women interviewed 97.4% of men identified and 97.7% of women identified as heterosexual.

A 2002 study by Monash University's Bob Birrell and Virginia Rapson also suggests that heterosexuality is the norm when concluding that same-sex couples only represent 0.47 of those Australians who are cohabitating.

A 2011 survey by the Australian Bureau of Statistics puts the figure of same-sex couples at 1%.

The figure quoted by the Safe Schools Coalition booklet, *Safe schools do better*, that approximately 16% of students are LGBTQI appears overstated given that the overwhelming majority of Australians describe themselves as heterosexual and the overwhelming majority of those with partners are also heterosexual.

No amount of LGBTQI gender theory can ever deny the fact that heterosexuality is the norm and that procreation is best served when women and men are involved.

One of the most disconcerting aspects of the debate about the Safe Schools Coalition program, and one that suggests the same-sex plebiscite is in danger of descending into personal abuse and vitriol, is the language often employed by LGBTQI advocates.

Those critical of the Safe Schools program are condemned as 'homophobic', 'transphobic' and 'heteronormative'. Bill Shorten, Leader of the Opposition, has gone as far as labelling those members of parliament critical of the program as "knuckle-dragging right-wing senators".

When releasing the Louden report and the Commonwealth Government's response Minister Birmingham argued that he had tried to set a middle course and that the suggested changes are reasonable and balanced. Such is the case as the Safe Schools Coalition program is still being federally funded and available to schools.

Left agenda slips under the cover

There's no doubt the Safe Schools Coalition program is more about lesbian, gay, bisexual, transgender, queer and intersex advocacy than addressing bullying in schools.

Victoria is where the program began and in 2006 the state's Department of Education and Training published an anti-bullying guide, Safe Schools are Effective Schools: A Resource for Developing Safe and Supportive School Environments.

Of the 29 pages of advice detailing types of bullying, its effect on students and what strategies schools should adopt to address the issue, one page dealt with strategies for responding to homophobic bullying.

Quite rightly, the booklet states: "All students, including gay, lesbian, bisexual, transgender and intersex students, in

Victorian government schools have the right to feel safe at school and be free from bullying."

Strategies suggested to address homophobic bullying included creating a safe and inclusive school environment where "everybody has the right to feel physically and psychologically safe".

Fast-forward to the Safe Schools Coalition program and it is obvious that there has been a quantum change. Instead of one page, we have a tsunami of material — hard copy and digital — championing "sexual diversity, intersex and gender diversity in schools".

The declaration in the Safe Schools Do Better booklet that the LGBTQI program "is proud to create change in schools" is a masterstroke in understatement. Materials associated with the program extol the positives associated with alternative gender and sexuality lifestyles without any mention of the risks.

According to the Safe Schools material, transgender people can be "lesbian, gay bisexual, queer, straight or something else". Welcome to the brave new world of gender diversity where biology no longer matters as one's gender is simply a sociocultural construct.

Anyone who considers the natural order of things to involve men and women is condemned as advocating "heterosexism", "homophobia" and "transphobia". For a supposed anti-bullying program, it is ironic that anyone expressing a preference for heterosexuality is attacked in such a way and made to feel guilty.

The bias evident in the Safe Schools Coalition program is further illustrated by its claim that the program is justified because 16% of students are same-sex attracted, gender diverse, trans or intersex.

Ignored is that Gender is Not Uniform, one of the publications recommended by the Safe Schools program, states: "It is currently very difficult to know exactly how many transgender and/or diverse young people there are in Australia."

In one of Australia's largest random-based surveys of sexual identity, carried out by Anthony Smith and Paul Badcock from La Trobe University, more than 97% of men and women aged 16 to 59 identified as heterosexual. Only 1.6% of men identified as gay and 0.9% as bisexual while 0.8% of women described themselves as lesbian and 1.4% as bisexual.

Research shows that puberty and adolescence are a time of experimentation and anxiety about gender and sexuality, but it is also clear that heterosexuality is the norm.

Although the All of Us booklet endorsed by the Safe Schools Coalition states: "Young people often realise they are lesbian, gay or bisexual between the ages of 11 and 14," ignored is the fact the overwhelming majority of young people, when they reach adulthood, identify as being male or female.

It also needs to be understood that the cultural-left ideology underpinning the Safe Schools Coalition's LGBTQI agenda has existed for many years.

In my book *Why Our Schools are Failing,* I cite the example of an academic arguing in 1994 that gender stereotypes must be deconstructed and that the English classroom should be "conceptualised as a socio-political site where alternative reading positions can be made available to students outside the oppressive male-female dualistic hierarchy — outside the oppressive phallogocentric signifying system of making meaning".

The Australian Education Union's 2003 policy on gay, lesbian, bisexual and transgender people states "homophobia and heterosexism must be included in the content of pre-service training for all teachers".

It argues "homosexuality and bisexuality need to be normalised and materials need to be developed (that) will help to combat homophobia".

The existence of the Safe Schools Coalition program illustrates how successful the cultural-left has been in taking the long march and forcing on schools its radical views about gender and sexuality.

Safe schools' rainbow is mostly red

The Commonwealth Governments Safe Schools Coalition program, directed at providing a more positive environment for "same sex attracted, intersex and gender diverse students" is being criticised for advocating radical views about gender and sexuality.

Senator Cory Bernardi from South Australia describes the program as indoctrinating "children into a Marxist agenda of cultural relativism". Senator Abetz from Tasmania argues that it is "a program of social engineering where parents, when they get to understand what it is, rebel against it and in fact vote for their schools not to be involved".

While there is no doubt that elements of the program involve a genuine attempt to reduce bullying and prejudice against Lesbian, Gay, Bisexual, Transgender, Queer and Intersex (LGBTQI) students Senators' Abetz and Bernardi are correct in what they argue.

The ideology underpinning the program and associated material reflects a cultural-left bias about gender and sexuality that has existed for many years. As I detailed in 'Why our schools are failing', published in 2004, the cultural-left has long argued that Western, capitalist society is 'phallocentric', 'oppressive' and 'misogynist'.

A rainbow alliance of cultural-left movements, including neo-Marxism, feminism, gender studies and queer theory argue that traditional views about sexuality and gender enforce a binary, hierarchal code that oppresses women and anyone who does not conform to society's heterosexist expectations.

Examples quoted in 'Why our schools are failing" include the University of Melbourne's History Department's course 'The Body: History, Sex and Gender' where students are introduced to: "an understanding of the different readings of the body... of the construction of the slender body, the gay and lesbian body, and the gendered body of the late 20th century".

At a national English teachers' conference, an academic, when referring to heterosexuality, argued: "I am proposing that this new form of hierarchical dualism can and should be resisted and challenged (by) using the English classroom as a site for resistance and interventionist strategies.

Central to LGBTQI ideology is the belief that heterosexuality is patriarchal and bourgeois and that men and boys have dominated for so long because of what the Italian Marxist Antonio Gramsci called hegemony.

Gramsci argues that unequal power relations within society occur because they appear natural and beyond dispute. Instead of gender being biologically determined it is a social construct and, as a result, students can be taught to act differently.

Drawing on the theories of the French Marxist Althusser the cultural-left also argues that schools are parts of the capitalist system's 'ideological state apparatus' and they must be critiqued and challenged if the socialist utopia is ever to arise.

As a result, the then South Australian school curriculum argued "gender is a social construction organised upon unequal power relations which define and limit opportunities for girls and boys… The current construction of the gender order also supports heterosexuality as the norm. Social constructions of advantage and disadvantage are of human making and therefore capable of change".

Given the history of gender and sexuality theory it should not surprise that the *Safe Schools do Better* booklet warns against heterosexism on the basis that it unfairly limits "ideas about what is 'normal' and 'not normal'". Reflecting Gramsci and Althusser the statement is also made that homophobia "includes institutional and cultural bias and structural inequality".

Not surprisingly, the Safe Schools Gender Questioning booklet adopts a relativistic position when telling students "There are many genders beyond just 'male' and 'female': gender can be fluid and limitless". The booklet goes on to tell students there "are no limitations on what your gender and identity can be".

While the Safe Schools Coalition argues that approximately 16% of students are LGBTQI it also must be accepted that while students, especially during puberty, might be uncertain about their sexuality and gender that by the time they enter the adult world they will be more comfortable with who and what they are.

Based on what is described as the "largest, most comprehensive population-based survey of sexuality ever undertaken in Australia" two researchers at La Trobe University's Research Centre in Sex, Health and Society conclude that approximately 98% of men and women identify as heterosexual.

In the context of the debate about same-sex marriage it is also important to note, according to the Australian Bureau of Statistics, that only 1% of couples describe themselves as same-sex.

Instead of acknowledging that heterosexuality is the norm in relation to Australian society the Safe Schools Coalition presents a negative caricature.

Nothing positive is presented about being heterosexual and in relation to the LGBTQI lifestyle there is no information about negatives such as the dangers of gender reassignment or the higher rates of HIV/AIDS.

Given events over the last two to three weeks it is obvious that the Safe Schools Coalition program is highly controversial and the Commonwealth Government is right to call for an inquiry.

LGBTQI schools program needs investigating

Is the Commonwealth government justified in reviewing the Safe Schools Coalition program directed at lessoning the impact of bullying by creating "safer and more inclusive educational environments for same sex attracted, intersex and gender diverse students, staff and families"?

According to a comment piece on the newmatilda.com website the answer is "no". Katherine Hudson argues that those expressing concerns about the program share the views of "many dictators, despots and despicable leaders, including Putin, Kim Jong-un, Mugabe, and ISIS terrorists".

So much for rational and sensible debate.

The reality is, though, based on an analysis of the program's resources, the answer is "yes". Instead of focusing on the problem of bullying the program is more about promoting a cultural-left LGBTQI agenda and presenting a negative view of heterosexuality.

The Coalition's booklet Safe Schools Do Better states that the program's intention is to support "sexual diversity, intersex and gender diversity in schools" and to "create change in schools".

To achieve this change teachers are asked to check whether their school has "anti-discrimination, bullying or diversity policies that explicitly name homophobia, transphobia and support for sexual and gender diversity".

Materials include posters, library resources, lesson plans and websites — many of which present a one-sided view of gender and sexuality that lacks the objectivity expected when dealing with such sensitive and often controversial matters.

Most parents would consider in the normal course of events that their children are either boys of girls but according to the Safe Schools Do Better booklet parents who do so are guilty of "heterosexism".

Heterosexism involves the assumption that "everyone is, or should be, heterosexual and that other types of sexuality or gender identity are unnatural or not as good as being heterosexual".

Ignored is the fact that believing sexuality involves a man and a woman does not equate with homophobia and transphobia and the reality, according to one study by researchers at La Trobe University, is that approximately 98% of women and men identify as heterosexual.

While the statistics quoted by the Safe Schools Coalition argues that 10% of students are same-sex attracted it also needs to be noted that an Australian survey carried out by Ray Morgan Research puts the figure at 4.6% of young people aged 14-19. The overwhelming majority of young people are heterosexual.

If the purpose of a union between a man and a woman is procreation then the physical reality is that heterosexuality is the norm and no amount of LGBTQI wishful thinking can make it otherwise.

In relation to gender, one of the Safe Schools' recommended resources argues that there are "many genders beyond just male and female" and that "gender can be fluid and limitless".

In relation to being transgender, the Gender Questioning booklet goes on to argue that trans people "have the same range of sexual orientations as the rest of the population and so could be lesbian, gay, bisexual, queer, straight or something else".

As to what "something else" might refer to is left unanswered but the booklet goes on to tell students that there "are no limitations on what your gender and identity can be". For those students wanting to undergo a gender transition process another booklet tells teachers, "It may be possible to consider a student a mature minor and able to make decisions without parental consent".

For those students who have undergone gender transition, with or without parental consent, the booklet titled *Guide To Supporting A Student To Affirm Or Transition Gender Identity At School* argues that sporting activities should not be segregated "on the basis of sex or gender identity".

The above booklet goes on to argue that schools should permit transgender students to use the "toilets, changing rooms, showers and swimming facilities based on the student's gender identity and the facilities they will feel most comfortable with".

The Safe Schools' *All Of Us* lesson plans for years 7 and 8 best illustrates how lacking in balance the program is. Under Program Aims the statement is made that the intention is to "create a school environment that recognises and celebrates the diversity of each person's unique sexuality, gender identity or intersex status".

Not unsurprisingly, nowhere in the booklet or in any other of the material examined is there anything positive said about heterosexuality. While the Safe Schools Coalition program seeks to promote tolerance and respect for diversity those students identifying as heterosexual are made to feel guilty and uncomfortable.

Lesson 4 of the *All of Us* booklet also presents a very stereotyped and misleading view of what it means to be male or female. Teachers are told that they should describe boys as being tough and not crying, wanting to watch action films and enjoying play fighting and wrestling.

Being female, on the other hand, involves cooking, enjoying shopping, wearing makeup, gossiping and enjoying dancing. Such a portrayal is simplistic and out of date in 21st century Australia where how men and women relate has become more complex and nuanced.

The La Trobe University's Australian Research Centre in Sex, Health and Society is one of the principal supporters of the Safe Schools Coalition and released a new resource titled *The Practical Guide to Love, Sex and Relationships.*

Similar to the Safe Schools Program the new material advocates a strong LGBTQI agenda. Directed at Years 7 to 10 students the material argues that society enforces gendered expectations (heterosexuality) that impact negatively on boys and girls.

Relationships and gender expectations between men and women are always negative while LGBTQI relationships are presented as always positive and beyond criticism.

One of the activities titled Freedom Fighters asks students to role play a situation where Martians invade and enforce a destructive binary code — where boys are boys and girls are girls. Students are then asked to be freedom fighters where the 'male' hero sings:

You don't have to be a certain way just because you have a penis
You don't have to be a certain way just because you have a vagina
We're not gonna care about that
We're gonna do what we wanna do
We're gonna be who we wanna be
I'm gonna lead you guys to victory and then I'm gonna go home
and enjoy my collection of vintage dolls
Because we're free, damn it
And they may take our penises
They may take our vaginas
But they will never take our freedom

Save school kids from radical views on sexuality

The decision by a mother to withdraw her son from Frankston High School because of the Safe Schools Coalition Program, where students are presented with material promoting a LGBTQI sexuality and gender agenda, highlights the issue of values and morality in schools.

The Safe Schools Coalition supports "sexual diversity, intersex and gender diversity in schools" under the banner of anti-bullying and is being implemented in schools across Australia with state, territory and Commonwealth funding.

Central to the program is the belief that a significant number of students are "same sex attracted, intersex and gender diverse" and that such students suffer from classrooms and schools where homophobia and transphobia are rife.

To further the cause of LGBTQI students the Coalition argues that schools should adopt a whole school approach involving surveys of staff and students, teaching materials, library resources, posters, Internet sites and professional learning packages.

The material argues that gender and sexuality are fluid concepts and that all forms of gender and sexuality should be treated equally. The belief that there are basically two sexes is condemned as "heterosexism" and students are told to celebrate diversity and difference.

One resource argues "there are many genders beyond 'male' or 'female'; gender can be fluid or limitless" and that "There are no rules about who you can be: all you need to do is be yourself".

Another resource tells teachers to "Challenge gender stereotypes and heteronormativity in discussions inside or outside the classroom" and to actively support "days of action and celebration such as the annual International Day Against Homophobia and Transphobia (IDAHOT)".

Schools are told that if boys identify as girls they should be allowed to participate in girls' sports and to use girls' toilets.

And it should be realised that schools being pressured to adopt a radical view of gender and sexuality has been ongoing for many years. The Australian Education Union's 2003 policy argues "Homosexuality and bisexuality need to be normalised and materials need to be developed which will help combat homophobia".

The AEU goes on to argue that "Any teacher-directed presentation or discussion of GLBT issues in a class situation should aim to be positive in its approach" and that teachers should be aware of the "sexual politics and the politics of health in order to deal with any prejudices, myths and superstitions which may exist".

For years, articles in the Australian Association for the Teaching of English have criticised literary texts like Romeo and Juliet, Pride and Prejudice and fairy tales like Cinderella for imposing gender categories that "are tied to an oppressive binary structure for organising the social and cultural practices of adolescent boys and girls".

While those students who identify as LGBTQI should not be unfairly discriminated against or victimised it is clear that the Safe Schools Coalition is more about advocacy than simply making schools safer places.

The fact that the Safe Schools Coalition's sexuality and gender program is endorsed by the Victorian education department and that an additional $1.04 million was allocated in the budget also shows that more and more schools will be expected to implement the program.

While presented as objective and impartial on reading the Safe Schools Coalition's material it is obvious students, under the guise of anti-bullying, are being subjected to a concerted and well-resourced campaign enforcing an LGBTQI sexuality and gender agenda.

Nowhere in the material is there any recognition that alternative sexual lifestyles or gender identities might be less than positive or less preferable to heterosexuality. To suggest otherwise it to be immediately labelled as homophobic, transphobic or guilty of heterosexism.

It is also the case that the Andrews Government and the Australian Education Union's support of the Safe Schools Coalition represents a glaring case of hypocrisy.

On one hand the teacher union argues that government schools must be secular and that there is no place for the type of morality and values associated with religion and the Andrews government has removed religious instruction classes from the formal school day.

Parents and schools are also told that Christian festivities should not be celebrated or promoted in government schools and the Australian Bishops are condemned for circulating to Catholic schools the *Don't Mess With Marriage* pastoral letter that argues marriage must involve a man and a woman.

At the same time the official government and education department policy is to ask schools to fully support the Safe Schools Coalition and its cultural-left agenda; one that is still controversial and far from settled in terms of the broader community.

All sides deserve a voice in same-sex marriage debate

While critics seek to punish the Catholic bishops for circulating their pastoral letter *Don't Mess With Marriage* to Catholic schools, by lodging a complaint with Tasmania's Anti-Discrimination Commissioner, there's no doubt supporters of same-sex marriage believe they have every right to promote their agenda in the nation's schools.

A December 2, 2015 article in *The Age*, a strong supporter of the LGBTQI (lesbian, gay, bisexual, transgender, queer or questioning, and intersex) view of marriage, encourages primary school children to listen to a new children's book, *The Gender Fairy*. The book celebrates the feelings of "transgender and non-binary children" and involves a "gender fairy (who is non-binary)" and the suggestion that it is OK for a young boy to use a male toilet and to wear girls' clothes.

A second example involves an *Age* article from September 17, 2015 about transgender students being discriminated against in areas such as "strict uniform rules, toilets, sports teams and even assumptions about subjects".

The article, after detailing the difficulties faced by transgender students in some schools, writes positively of the situation in which "mature minors can make decisions to affirm their gender identity at school, even if their parents disagree".

A third example involves an August 31, 2015 *Age* editorial arguing against the decision of the NSW government to ban showing the pro-same-sex marriage film *Gayby Baby* during school hours.

The editorial argues that same-sex marriages are "normal", that not showing the film is an example of "bigotry and injustice", and that it should be shown in all Victorian secondary schools.

The Australian Education Union's policy on gay, lesbian, bisexual, transgender, queer or questioning, and intersex people also supports enforcing the LGBTQI agenda in schools when arguing "Sexuality should be included in all curriculum relating to health and personal development. Homosexuality, bisexuality, transgenderism and intersex need to be normalised."

The AEU policy also warns against the "pervasive assumption of heterosexuality which is common to language, the law and other institutions in society e.g. the education system and the family" and argues that "Educational Institutions must implement strategies to counter homophobia, biphobia, transphobia, heterosexism and monosexism".

The Safe Schools Coalition, funded by state and commonwealth governments and being implemented across many of the nation's schools, is also based on the premise that advocates of same-sex marriage and the LGBTQI gender agenda have every right to promulgate their values and beliefs.

Material on The Safe Schools Coalition website tells school children that there is nothing natural or unique about heterosexual marriage and that "Australian and international research shows that it is the quality of parenting relationships that determines a child's wellbeing, not their family structure".

The Safe Schools Coalition also argues that those who favour heterosexual marriage are guilty of imposing "a hierarchy where attitudes and practices that affirm heterosexuality are seen as better than those that don't. For example, believing that marriage should only be between a man and a woman is a heteronormative view."

It should be understood that those advocating an LGBTQI gender and sexuality agenda in schools have been doing so for some time. At a 1994 national English teachers conference, writer Maria Pallotta-Chiarolli, from South Australia, argued that the English classroom had to be used "as a site for resistance and interventionist strategies" to deal with "homophobia and AIDS-phobia".

In a gender-equity booklet *So What's a Boy?* published at the same time, Canadian educator Wayne Martino argued that the English classroom had to be "conceptualised as a socio-political site where alternative reading positions can be made available to students outside of an oppressive male-female dualistic hierarchy - outside of an oppressive phallogocentric signifying system for making meaning".

Not to be outdone, a 1995 resource for primary schools developed by the Curriculum Corporation, titled *Fractured Fairytales,* argued that teachers must "challenge stereotyping and sexist language in traditional literature" by questioning tales such as *Cinderella* and *Jack and the Beanstalk*.

That advocates of same-sex marriage and an LGBTQI agenda have been given, and continue to be given, free reign in promoting their agenda in state and territory schools is beyond doubt. Also beyond doubt is that those seeking to put a counter view, such as the Australian bishops with their pastoral letter *Don't Mess With Marriage*, are being denied the same opportunity to advocate their beliefs about what constitutes marriage.

In what is supposedly an open and free society, where freedom of religion and freedom of expression are guaranteed by state, national and international covenants and agreements, such a situation is hypocritical and intolerable.

Hypocritical because those advocating change refuse to allow those they disagree with the same right to express a point of view. Intolerable in that the shortest route to a totalitarian state is to deny freedom of speech and freedom of religion.

Ancient institution of marriage cannot be meaningfully redefined

The vote in Ireland has intensified debates in Australian about redefining marriage to include same-sex relationships and there's no doubt that the issue will be addressed by the Commonwealth parliament sooner rather than later.

Debates about same-sex marriage must be seen in the broader context of marriage as one of society's most enduring and beneficial institutions. Since the dawn of time and in all societies, cultures and major religions marriage involving a heterosexual relationship has been preeminent.

In October, 2014 the Catholic Church held a Synod on the Family at the Vatican in which Pope Francis called on the assembly of Bishops to discuss the institution of marriage within the Church.

The Synod's final report discusses the numerous challenges faced by families and the increasing pressure on matrimony as one of the key sacraments of the Church.

There's no doubt that traditional ideas about the nature of marriage and its place in Western cultures are changing dramatically.

Before the Cultural Revolution of the late '60s is was socially and morally unacceptable for men and women to cohabit unless they were married and divorce was considered as the last resort.

The Cultural Revolution, epitomised by hippies and flower power, the anti-war movement and the mantra 'make love, not war', undermined the status quo in institutions like marriage and those who had been radicalised argued for alternative lifestyles.

Books like *The Female Eunuch*, by Germaine Greer, argued that marriage was a form of oppression, with some feminists describing marriage as a form of sexual exploitation and enslavement.

In Australia in 1975 the institution of marriage was also weakened by the introduction of non-fault divorce by the Whitlam Labor Government that made it far easier to break the bonds of matrimony.

The way marriage is treated in the school curriculum provides additional evidence that conservative ideas about marriage (involving a man and a woman in a sacred and lasting relationship with the purpose of having children) have changed significantly.

Primary children are taught that marriage can involve a man and a woman or two people of the same-sex and that it is wrong to judge either type of union as preferable.

As a result of changing social mores and no-fault divorce, fewer people have married and divorce rates have increased. It is also true that the rise of single parent families and the absence of biological fathers have led to increased rates of child abuse.

Evidence that the benefits of being freed from supposedly old fashioned and inflexible definition of marriage have failed to materialise is detailed in *Maybe 'I do': modern marriage & the pursuit of happiness* by Kevin Andrews, the Defence Minister in the Commonwealth government at the time of writing.

Andrews argues: "a healthy, stable and happy marriage is an optimal relationship for the psychological, emotional and physical wellbeing of adults and children".

What's to be done? The first step is to acknowledge that same-sex couples are already fully protected under the law. Couples share all the protections offered by marriage in areas like superannuation, sharing property and other legal and financial arrangements.

Secondly, we need to evaluate the impact changes in the definition of marriage are having on families and society. If re-defining the institution of marriage is counter-productive then the facts must be revealed.

Thirdly, the school curriculum should no longer adopt a morally relativistic approach to what constitutes marriage and students should not be indoctrinated with cultural-left views about gender and sexuality.

Religious leaders and institutions also need to stress the sanctity of marriage and the moral obligation it places on all of those involved. In a narcissistic culture consumed by what is transitory, marriage is symbolised by a higher sense of purpose and deeper commitment between a man and a woman.

As observed by His Holiness Pope Francis: "Marriage now tends to be viewed as a form of mere emotional satisfaction that can be constructed in any way or modified at will. But the indispensable contribution of marriage to society transcends the feelings and momentary needs of the couple".

Finally, it has to be realised that defining marriage as between same-sex couples involves what in philosophy is known as a category mistake. In the same way it is impossible to describe night as day or day as night it is impossible to define marriage as anything else but the life-long union of a women and a man for the purpose of having children.

No amount of legislation or referendums will alter the fact that while same-sex couples can share love and companionship their relationship bears no resemblance to marriage as it is defined.

Camille's gender agenda

Read the American feminist Camille Paglia's latest book *Free Women Free Men Sex Gender and Feminism* and it's easy to understand why she is so hated and loathed by the sisterhood. Paglia, who describes herself as a "non-gendered entity", criticises mainstream feminists for being drab and puritanical and argues it's OK for women to be feminine and alluring.

Her heroines include the sultry, glamorous movie actress Lauren Bacall and the pop diva Madonna. Paglia also writes how she admires assertive and confident women like the aviatrix Amelia Earhart who had the confidence to succeed without playing the gender card.

At a time when so many young women are being pressured to gain a career and succeed professionally Paglia argues the danger is that the biological clock is ticking and that it is wrong to suggest those who choose motherhood instead of a career are "wasting their talents".

The reality is that those women who leave it to too long to conceive face obstacles and those lucky enough to have children face the difficulties and challenges of balancing both being a mother and a career woman.

While there is no doubt that harassing or abusing a woman is totally unacceptable and sexual predators like the Hollywood director Harvey Weinstein, if convicted, must be punished Paglia also argues that it is wrong to stereotype and demonise men as sexist and misogynist.

Paglia describes feminist attacks on men as "peevish", "unpalatable" and "unjust" as not all men abuse or mistreat women. She also makes the point that "if women seek freedom, they must let men too be free".

Important is this regard is giving boys strong male role medals when in primary school and not emasculating them as they grow older by feminising the curriculum and making them feel guilty about being male.

Proven by Marxist inspired programs like Safe Schools, where children are told gender is fluid and limitless and they can decide for themselves whether they are male or female or any of the other 26 categories in between, it's clear that radical gender theory now dominates western societies.

And it's here, once again, that Paglia refuses to be politically correct. Instead of gender being a matter of choice where individuals can self-identify she argues the "DNA of every cell of the human body is inflexibly coded as male or female from birth to death".

Sounding much like the past head of the Australian Christian Lobby Lyle Shelton, Paglia also argues that radical gender

advocates like Roz Ward who designed the Safe Schools program are guilty of pushing "propaganda" when arguing gender is a social construct.

The reality is that genetics and hormones are biological facts that determine who and what we are.

As a result, like the Australian feminist Germaine Greer who was condemned as transphobic for arguing that a man who has undergone a sex reassignment can never be a woman, Paglia is also attacked for criticising what she describes as the "extravaganza of gender experimentation".

Whereas our universities were once bastions of free speech and open debate and inquiry in America, England and Australia they have fallen victim to political correctness where anyone who dares to question the prevailing orthodoxy in areas like gender, sexuality, race and the environment is vilified and attacked.

Paglia describes this as "intolerance masquerading as tolerance and where individual liberty is crushed by the tyranny of the group". Australian examples include the eminent historian Geoffrey Blainey being forced out of Melbourne University and the University of Western Australia cancelling the appointment of climate sceptic Bjorn Lomborg.

The University of New South Wales now has a Diversity Kit that tells students and lecturers they must embrace 'Cultural Diversity and Inclusive Practice'. Examples include telling students that Australia was 'invaded' and that it is wrong to suggest Captain Cook discovered Australia.

As noted by Paglia the end result is that robust and

independent academic debate is silenced by political correctness and identity politics where all those who self-identify as
victims are treated as snow-flakes.

Central to Paglia's philosophy is the belief that as a result
of nature and human biology men and women are essentially
different. After years of study and investigation she concludes
"that there is something fundamentally constant in gender that
is grounded in concrete facts".

Only women menstruate and are fashioned to conceive and
bear children and are best placed to care for and raise their
children when young. Men can never be pregnant and have no
understanding or appreciation of what it means to experience
child birth.

While feminists seek to create a world where gender and
sexuality no longer define men and women Paglia also argues
that the two sexes can be equal while different.

She writes "what is indispensable is that women do not gain
by weakening men. An enlightened feminism… can only be
built upon a wary alliance of strong women and strong men".